Guide to Motor Insurers' Bureau

Other titles available from Law Society Publishing:

Criminal Injuries Compensation Claims 2008
Laura Begley, Aileen Downey and Clare Padley

Titles from Law Society Publishing can be ordered from all good bookshops or direct (telephone 0870 850 1422, email **lawsociety@prolog.uk.com** or visit our online shop at **bookshop.lawsociety.org.uk**).

GUIDE TO MOTOR INSURERS' BUREAU CLAIMS

10TH EDITION

Donald B. Williams and Malcolm Johnson

The Law Society

Crown copyright material is reproduced with the permission of the Controller of Her Majesty's Stationery Office.
MIB material is reproduced with the kind permission of the Motor Insurers' Bureau.

ISBN-13: 978-1-907698-65-1

Originally published in 1969 by Oyez Publishing under the title
The Motor Insurers' Bureau
Eighth edition published in 2000 by Blackstone Press Ltd
Ninth edition published in 2003 by the Law Society

This tenth edition published in 2012 by the Law Society
113 Chancery Lane, London WC2A 1PL

Typeset by Columns Design Ltd, Reading
Printed by Hobbs the Printers Ltd, Totton, Hants

The paper used for the text pages of this book is FSC® certified. FSC (the Forest Stewardship Council®) is an international network to promote responsible management of the world's forests.

Contents

APPENDICES

Foreword

There cannot be many solicitors who have practices that at some time do not require them to have knowledge of matters covered by the Motor Insurer's Bureau (MIB). This outstanding book will provide invaluable assistance as it sets out clearly and cogently the important role of the MIB as well the circumstances in which a victim can make a claim from it.

Since the ninth edition was produced there have been many developments, including two supplementary agreements in 2008 and 2011 for untraced drivers and a supplementary agreement in 2008 for uninsured drivers. Details of these agreements and the relevant EC directives are explained clearly and cogently in this book.

Any lawyer consulted about claims against uninsured or untrained drivers will find this book an invaluable first point of call and it is highly unlikely that it will not produce the appropriate answer. A particularly impressive feature of this comprehensive text is its clear writing style and its sensible use of chapter headings and sub-headings. All in all it is a model of clarity. This is particularly important in an area in which the law is complex as that covered by the MIB.

I have no hesitation in commending this excellent book which I believe to be indispensible for practitioners.

Justice Stephen Silber
September 2012

Preface to the 10th edition

I began the first edition of this book in 1969. Little did I know then that I would still be around and be involved in a 10th edition! It was my original intention to provide for myself, as well as for others, mainly solicitors and barristers and Legal Advice Centres, to have at hand a little book on the shelf to be of some help, in easily understandable form, to get to grips with the terms of the formal Motor Insurers' Bureau Agreements in force, as well as the way in which the Bureau had applied them in practice, with a summary of relevant case law, along with a few practical hints to those pursuing claims.

It has been a pleasurable task for me to update the Guide over the past 43 years while I was still in practice as a litigation partner in a London West End firm and after 1976 when I was appointed a recorder and a full-time judge of the Employment Tribunal, and since my retirement.

In the preface to the ninth edition I welcomed the invaluable assistance of Malcolm Johnson, a practising solicitor specialising in Motor Insurers' Bureau claims among other types of claim and with a reputation as a lecturer and writer on such topics. It is, therefore, with much pleasure that I am able at least once more to thank him for his much more substantial contribution.

My hope, as always, has been to continue to provide a useful and handy guide to practitioners and others.

Donald B. Williams
September 2012

About the authors

Donald Williams qualified as a solicitor in 1955 and he is now retired. He was a litigation partner in a London West End firm until his appointment as a judge of the Employment Tribunal in 1976. He was also appointed a Recorder of the Crown Court and held other judicial appointments, including sitting on the Criminal Injuries Compensation Appeals Panel. The first edition of *The Motor Insurers' Bureau* was published in 1969. He has also lectured at the University of Buckingham and at Ashridge and Henley Management Colleges. Apart from writing books and articles on a variety of aspects of law, he is also the author of a selection published as *On the Lighter Side of the Law* (B. Rose, 1981).

After retiring, Donald was appointed a trustee and director of Barnet Citizens Advice Bureau. He lives with his wife, Judy, in north-west London and is a keen amateur musician.

Malcolm Johnson qualified as a solicitor in 1994 and he works as an associate solicitor for Blake Lapthorn in London. He is a Fellow of the Association of Personal Injury Lawyers, a member of the Law Society's Personal Injury Panel, a member of the Society of Trusts and Estates Practitioners and, since 2010, a solicitor advocate.

Malcolm is a co-author of *Child Abuse Compensation Claims*, published by Jordans, as well as a contributor to the *Encyclopaedia of Insurance Law*, published by Sweet and Maxwell, and *Personal Injury – Practice and Precedents*, published by Jordans. Malcolm has written numerous articles on the subject of personal injury law and he has lectured for the Association of Personal Injury Lawyers and Central Law Training.

Malcolm lives with his wife, Judith, in Mole Valley and is a keen runner and horse-rider.

Table of cases

Table of statutes

Table of statutory instruments

Table of European legislation

Abbreviations

APIL	Association of Personal Injury Lawyers
Bureau	Motor Insurers' Bureau (or MIB)
CICA	Criminal Injuries Compensation Authority
CICAP	Criminal Injuries Compensation Appeals Panel
CJEU	Court of Justice of the European Community
DVLA	Driver and Vehicle Licensing Agency
EC	European Community
ECJ	European Court of Justice
EEA	European Economic Area
MIB	Motor Insurers' Bureau (or Bureau)
MIBI	Motor Insurers' Bureau of Ireland
MID	Motor Insurance Database
MIIC	Motor Insurers' Information Centre
RTA 1988	Road Traffic Act 1988
SORN	Statutory Off Road Notification

CHAPTER 1

Introduction

1.1 GAPS IN THE LAW

By the time the 'roaring twenties' in the twentieth century had come to a close, horseless vehicles had already roared past the stage of development that rendered them capable of being extremely dangerous. It was against this background that the Road Traffic Act 1930 came into being. Indeed, one purpose of the Act, as stated in the Preamble, was 'to make provision for the protection of third parties against risks arising out of the use of motor vehicles'. Even though it may not have been fully realised at the time, it soon became apparent that there were certain types of risk for which there was no protection either under the Act or at all.

Thus, the 1930 Act gave no redress when a claim, rightly brought by someone who had sustained injuries as a result of a motorist's negligent driving, could not be, or otherwise was not, met, for some good reason, by the motorist or his or her insurers. Among this class of case were cases in which the motorist at fault became, or was already, without means.

Some claims failed because a second or third motorist would drive off after a 'cutting-in' manoeuvre, leaving behind injured victims and damaged cars. The victim(s) would not normally have any information capable of leading to the discovery of the identity of the driver concerned and would thus not be in a position to bring proceedings.

Other examples arose out of incomplete insurance cover, for instance, where the policy covered the motorist only for accidents arising in the course of his or her trade, and the particular accident occurred while the vehicle was being driven for social purposes (or vice versa).

Yet another illustration would be when the motorist had persuaded his or her insurers to provide a policy on the basis of some false statement or omission in the answers on the proposal form, thus negating the cover. One could, of course, add to these examples. The more important types of cases will be dealt with in greater detail below.

The 1930 Act is due to be replaced by the Third Parties (Rights Against Insurers) Act 2010, which will give enhanced rights to claimants. However, at the time of writing, this Act has not yet been brought into force.

1.2 THE CASSEL COMMITTEE

In brief, while the Road Traffic Act 1930 made insurance against third party claims compulsory, there was no provision in that Act, or elsewhere, for third parties to be compensated where the motorist had been negligent and was not covered, for some reason or another, by a policy of insurance. Arising from this situation, a committee to consider compulsory insurance was set up under the chairmanship of Sir Felix Cassel KC. It comprised lawyers as well as insurers. The *Report of the Committee on Compulsory Insurance* came out in July 1937, and contained the following conclusions:

1.   Where a claim was established against an uninsured motorist by a third party, the third party should have the right to recover from a central fund.
2.   Where a motorist was unable to meet a claim brought by a third party, the same right should be available.
3.   Where, however, a negligent motorist could not be traced (the 'hit-and-run' type of case), it was feasible to extend a right to recover from a central fund.
4.   Provision should be made for a solvency test of insurance companies to be administered by a Board of Trade, which would have power to grant or withhold a licence to carry on business as an insurer, and for a fund to be set up as a 'second line of defence' to meet claims due to be paid by insurance companies that became insolvent.

1.3 ESTABLISHMENT OF THE MOTOR INSURERS' BUREAU AND THE AGREEMENTS

With a view to implementing *some* of the conclusions reached by the Cassel Committee, what has been described as 'an entirely novel piece of extra-statutory machinery' was set up with the co-operation of the major insurers. On 31 December 1945, the Minister of War Transport and the companies and Lloyd's syndicates dealing with motor insurance in this country entered into an agreement.

Provision was made in that agreement for the establishment of a fund to be administered by a body known as the Motor Insurers' Bureau, and to which we will refer in this book as either the 'MIB' or the 'Bureau'.

The main object of the agreement was to implement the recommendation of the Cassel Committee to provide for compensation for victims of accidents occurring on the road where no compensation was available, or recoverable, due to the absence, or non-effectiveness of insurance cover of the driver to blame for the accident. The agreement did not seek to fill any other of the 'gaps' outlined.

The MIB is a company incorporated under the Companies Act 1929. Pursuant to an undertaking given by representatives of the companies dealing with motor insurance in this country, the parties to the original Motor Insurers' Bureau Agreement were the Ministry of Transport and the Bureau. The present situation is that the

MIB acts on behalf of the UK government to compensate victims of road accidents caused by uninsured or untraced drivers and it deals with over 30,000 claims every year from victims involved in accidents with uninsured and hit-and-run drivers.

The following is a chronology of how the original MIB Agreement has been supplemented and replaced by other Agreements over the years.

1. The first MIB Agreement dated 17 June 1946 applied to uninsured drivers, although the MIB could give 'sympathetic' consideration to claims made by victims of untraced drivers. This applied to claims arising in respect of an incident occurring between 1 July 1946 and 28 February 1971.

2. On 21 April 1969, the first Agreement for untraced driver claims was made, placing an obligation on the MIB to meet claims arising out of 'hit-and-run' accidents occurring between 1 May 1969 and 30 November 1972.

3. On 1 February 1971, an Agreement was made for uninsured drivers only, relating to accidents occurring on or after 1 March 1971 and before 1 December 1972. This replaced the 1946 Agreement. The 1971 Agreement was replaced in turn by a new Agreement dated 22 November 1972 relating to accidents occurring on or after 1 December 1972 and before 31 December 1988.

4. On 22 November 1972, an Agreement was made for untraced drivers relating to accidents occurring on or after 1 December 1972 and before 1 July 1996.

5. On 7 December 1977, a Supplementary Agreement was made for untraced driver claims relating to accidents occurring on or after 3 January 1978 and before 1 July 1996.

6. On 21 December 1988, an Agreement was made for uninsured driver claims for accidents occurring on or after 31 December 1988 and before 1 October 1999. This superseded the 1972 Agreement.

7. On 14 June 1996, an Agreement was made for untraced driver claims in respect of accidents occurring on or after 1 July 1996.

8. On 13 August 1999, an Agreement was made for uninsured driver claims for accidents occurring on or after 1 October 1999.

9. On 7 February 2003, an Agreement was made for untraced driver claims for accidents occurring on or after 14 February 2003.

10. On 7 November 2008, a Supplementary Agreement was made for uninsured driver claims for accidents occurring on or after 7 November 2008.

11. On 30 December 2008, a Supplementary Agreement was made for untraced driver claims for accidents occurring on or after 1 February 2009.

12. On 15 April 2011, a second Supplementary Agreement was made for untraced driver claims for accidents occurring on or after 15 April 2011.

There are also two Memoranda of Understanding, the first dealing with the effect of *Byrne (a Minor)* v. *The Motor Insurers' Bureau and the Secretary of State for Transport* [2008] EWCA Civ 574 on claims under the Untraced Drivers' Agreement and the second following the implementation of the Fifth Motor Insurance Directive (2005/14/EC), which removes the excess payable by the claimant under the 1999 Uninsured Drivers' Agreement.

The 1999 Uninsured Drivers' Agreement and the 2003 Untraced Drivers' Agreement (as supplemented by the 2008 and 2011 Supplementary Agreements described above) are the current Agreements. Practitioners should note that these Agreements apply to 'Great Britain' which is England, Wales and Scotland. Separate agreements exist for Northern Ireland and the Crown Dependencies (the Channel Islands and Gibraltar).

In addition, both Agreements have 'Notes' at the end for further guidance. The Notes for Guidance to the 1999 Agreement were amended as from 15 April 2002. Any claims made under the 1999 Agreement on or after 15 April 2002 are handled by the MIB in accordance with the amended Notes for Guidance.

The text of the current Agreements and the Supplementary Agreements is reproduced in the Appendices. Copies may also be obtained from the MIB website (**www.mib.org.uk**) in the Downloadable Documents section. These were formerly obtainable from The Stationery Office (which took over the functions of Her Majesty's Stationery Office) at **www.tsoshop.co.uk** but it appears that they are now out of print.

The Agreements were also published on the Directgov website (**www.direct. gov.uk**) and can still be found on archived web pages using an internet search. However, practitioners need to exercise caution as to which version they consult. Both the MIB and Directgov website (recently replaced by **www.gov.uk**) published the Revised Notes for Guidance to the 1999 Uninsured Drivers' Agreement, but on the Directgov website they were reproduced separately with a legal notice at the top. At the same time, the 2003 Untraced Drivers' Agreement published on the MIB website does not contain any Notes for Guidance, whereas the version that appeared on the Directgov website did. Furthermore, there is a typographical error in para.2(c) of the Schedule to the original 2003 Untraced Drivers' Agreement which appears on the MIB website, which was corrected on the Directgov website version (see **Chapter 3**).

One of the most common causes of professional negligence claims against practitioners in this area of the law arises out of a failure to read the original text of the Agreements.

The present address of the MIB is Motor Insurers' Bureau, Linford Wood House, 6-12 Capital Drive, Linford Wood, Milton Keynes, MK14 6XT, DX: 142620 Milton Keynes 10 (tel: 01908 830001; email: enquiries@mib.org.uk). The present chief executive is Mr Ashton West. It should be noted that the MIB's present address has changed from the address set out in the 1999 Agreement.

1.4 EUROPEAN MOTOR INSURANCE DIRECTIVES

Since the UK became a full member of the European Community in 1972, its law has been shaped by various Directives issued by the European Commission. Some of these Directives are intended to promote the free movement of goods and services throughout the Community, and harmonise the road traffic laws in various Member States. The European Commission has issued six main Directives relating to motor insurance. These have defined not only the liability of insurers, but also the liability of the MIB. Typically, Member States are given a period of time in which to implement the Directives by way of statutes or statutory instruments. However, the Directives may mean a change to the MIB Agreements. By way of example, the latest Supplementary Uninsured and Untraced Drivers' Agreements are the government's response to case law and the Fifth Motor Insurance Directive.

The Directives are important because where there is a dispute as to the interpretation of motor insurance law (including the MIB Agreements), in certain circumstances the court can look back at the terms of the Directive from which that law flows. Moreover, the Directives are sometimes implemented late, or implemented incorrectly. A claimant might thus be able either (a) to rely on the terms of the original Directive or (b) to sue the UK government for not implementing the Directive. Over the years, the courts (not only in this jurisdiction but also in other jurisdictions within the European Community) have identified a number of conflicts between domestic road traffic legislation and the terms of the Directives. Consequently, practitioners should have some familiarity with what the Directives say and be aware of potential conflicts. We will be looking at cases where some of these conflicts have been examined by the courts in later chapters of this book.

The Directives make reference to the European Community (EC) and the European Economic Area (EEA). The EC is composed of the countries listed on the Europa website, which can be found at **www.europa.eu/about-eu/countries**. The EEA consists of the Member States of the EC and three of the four states of the European Free Trade Association, currently Iceland, Norway and Liechtenstein.

Each Directive begins with a series of 'recitals' which set out the purposes of the Directive. These are followed by 'articles' which direct each Member State within the EC on the measures that it needs to take to achieve those purposes.

The six main Motor Insurance Directives are listed below:

1. The First Motor Insurance Directive (72/166/EEC) made third party insurance compulsory throughout the EC. It also required Member States to ensure that motor vehicles 'normally based' in their territory were covered by compulsory civil liability insurance that would also cover loss or injury sustained in another Member State.

2. The Second Motor Insurance Directive (84/5/EEC) required each Member State to ensure that it had set up a 'body' to guarantee a minimum amount of compensation for victims of uninsured and untraced drivers. However, Member States were allowed to exclude from the payment of compensation

'persons who voluntarily entered the vehicle … [when] they knew that it was uninsured'. It also allowed for the exclusion of property damage in unidentified vehicle claims and the application of an excess in uninsured vehicle claims.

3. The Third Motor Insurance Directive (90/232/EEC) sought to improve the rights of road traffic accident victims. It forbade the national guarantee fund (the MIB) to require a claimant to prove that the defendant could not pay compensation. It further provided that Member States should oblige insurers or the guarantee fund (i.e. the MIB) to compensate victims of road traffic accidents, leaving any adjustment between the insurer and the Bureau to be sorted out later. Motor insurance policies were required to cover the whole of the EC.

4. The Fourth Motor Insurance Directive (2000/26/EC) aimed to give an injured party a direct right of action against the insurer. It also obliged insurance companies to set up 'information centres' to make it easier for claimants to locate a driver's insurer. Insurance companies were also required to appoint 'claims representatives' throughout the EEA and set out time limits for insurance companies and their claims representatives to respond to claims as well as penalties for their failure to do so. Finally, it provided that Member States should set up a national compensation body if an insurance company or a claims representative failed to deal with a claimant's claim.

5. The Fifth Motor Insurance Directive (2005/14/EC) set out a number of provisions, including:

    (a) compensation for accident victims where vehicles had false or no registration plates;

    (b) an increase in the minimum compulsory insurance limits and a mechanism to review those limits every five years. The new limit is €1,000,000 for personal injury or €5,000,000 whatever the number of victims. In the case of property damage, the minimum cover is €1,000,000;

    (c) an obligation on Member States to take the measures necessary to ensure that any statutory provision or any contractual clause contained in an insurance policy which excluded a passenger from such cover on the basis that he or she knew, or should have known, that the driver of the vehicle was under the influence of alcohol or of any other intoxicating agent at the time of an accident, should be deemed void in respect of the claims of any such passenger;

    (d) liability towards pedestrians and cyclists;

    (e) abolition of the Bureau's 'excess' in uninsured driver claims;

    (f) restrictions on the right of the Bureau to limit or exclude the payment of compensation in the event of damage to property by an unidentified vehicle;

    (g) improved insurance cover for persons who stay temporarily in another Member State;

(h)   an obligation on insurers to provide a 'statement relating to third party liability claims' if the insured wished to go to a new insurer;

(i)   an extension of the direct right of action by the injured victims against an insurer so that they were not confined to the circumstances set out in the Fourth Motor Insurance Directive;

(j)   an extension of the role of the information centres so that they were not confined to the type of accidents referred to in the Fourth Motor Insurance Directive.

6.   The Sixth Motor Insurance Directive (2009/103/EC) consolidates and clarifies the First to the Fifth Motor Insurance Directives.

1.5   MOTOR INSURANCE DATABASE AND THE MOTOR INSURERS' INFORMATION CENTRE

The Motor Insurance Database (MID) and the Motor Insurers' Information Centre (MIIC) were launched in 2001 to tackle the problems of uninsured driving. The MIIC is the organisation which collects and disseminates information relating to insurance details for registered vehicles.

The Motor Vehicles (Compulsory Insurance) (Information Centre and Compensation Body) Regulations 2003, SI 2003/37, implements some of the terms of the Fourth Motor Insurance Directive and extends the right to insurance information for injured parties involved in domestic traffic accidents (i.e. those occurring within the UK). A claimant or his or her representative is entitled to search the MID by making an application in writing or online.

The 2003 Regulations also oblige the MIIC to co-operate with corresponding information centres in other EEA countries. Practically speaking, this means that if a claimant is injured in an accident abroad within the EEA, he or she can approach the MIB to find out the claims representative of the liable insurer or obtain the information online from the **www.midis.org.uk** website.

The MID contains details of 35 million insured vehicles in the UK. Both the police and the Driver and Vehicle Licensing Agency (DVLA) have access to the MID. The police are able to make use of Automatic Number Plate Recognition technology to identify a vehicle that may be uninsured. They have been given extensive powers to seize uninsured vehicles under the Serious Organised Crime and Police Act 2005. The MIB's 2011 Annual Report stated that the MIB had assisted the police in removing 149,293 uninsured vehicles from the road through database enquiries.

Practitioners should be aware that, at present, an entry on the MID is not conclusive either of insurance or lack of insurance. Furthermore, the search for insurance is based on the number plate of the vehicle involved in the accident, not the individual driving the car, who might conceivably be covered by his or her own 'driving other cars' insurance.

The MIB's 2010 Annual Report also stated that it had settled 61,360 claims in that year and its annual levy (the amount that it requires from its member insurers) was £317.2 million. However, the MIB states on its website that the number of claims is falling. In addition, its 2011 Annual Report states that, for the three years to 2011, the annual levy on its members was actually reducing. £140 million was also returned from its central funds to insurer members in 2010 and 2011.

While the MID together with the efforts made by the police and DVLA have reduced the incidence of uninsured drivers by 25 per cent over the last three years, the MIB says that the incidence of uninsured driving remains 'stubbornly high'. It highlights the rather chilling statistic that about 900,000 drivers under the age of 30 are currently driving without insurance. The MIB further estimates that uninsured and untraced drivers kill about 100 people a year and injure another 23,000. That is a huge cost in human terms, quite apart from the bill for the insurance industry, and ultimately for those who pay insurance premiums.

In addition, the Motor Vehicles (Insurance Requirements) Regulations 2011, SI 2011/20, introduced regulations in support of the offence of being the registered keeper of a vehicle which does not have insurance cover (Road Traffic Act 1988, s.144A). The Regulations came into force on 4 February 2011. There is now a continuous insurance enforcement scheme, which compels all vehicle owners to insure their vehicles whether they are on, or off, the road. The alternative is to make a Statutory Off Road Notification (SORN) to the DVLA. There are, unfortunately, a huge number of people who drive uninsured vehicles, but they can only be caught when they are behind the wheel. It is hoped that the continuous insurance enforcement scheme will reduce those numbers still further.

1.6 PROCEDURE FOR CLAIMING

It should be borne in mind that the MIB is not a court of law nor is it a tribunal. However, it does require claims under both the Uninsured and Untraced Drivers' Agreements to be submitted on forms it provides. The forms are designed to produce the full range of relevant evidence necessary to support the claim. Such evidence must be present in the form required and additional evidence may be required by the MIB. Practitioners should always make sure that they check the MIB's website for the current forms.

Clause 19 of the 1999 Uninsured Drivers' Agreement provides a mechanism whereby a claimant may refer any dispute 'as to the reasonableness of a requirement made by the MIB for the supply of information or documentation or for the taking of any step' to the Secretary of State. The authors are not aware of any case where a claimant has relied upon this clause. However, as will be seen later in this book, issues such as the interpretation of various clauses in the Uninsured Drivers' Agreement together with the reasonableness of information requirements set by the MIB are adjudicated upon by the courts. (See **Chapter 2**.)

Clause 28 of the 2003 Untraced Drivers' Agreement contains a procedure by which any dispute between the claimant and the MIB 'concerning a decision, determination or requirement made by MIB under the terms of [the 2003] Agreement [other than a determination arising under clause 18] shall be referred to and determined by an arbitrator'. However, again, as will be seen later on in this book, such issues can end up before the domestic courts in Great Britain and the European Court of Justice.

CHAPTER 2

Uninsured driver claims

2.1 INTRODUCTION

In cases where the offending motorist is not insured, the victim of an accident may still bring proceedings to recover damages for personal injuries. Since 1946, when the first Motor Insurers' Bureau Agreement came into operation, the Bureau has paid to successful claimants any sums due under the judgment, including costs, where the judgment is unsatisfied within seven days.

With the 1988 Agreement, the Bureau's liabilities were extended to damage to property (principally other vehicles, but also damage caused by crashing into a house, for example, or knocking over a bus stop).

The 1999 Uninsured Drivers' Agreement applies to accidents on or after 1 October 1999. It is accompanied by 'Notes for the Guidance of Victims of Road Traffic Accidents', which were revised for accidents on or after 15 April 2002. However, it is unclear how far these Revised Notes for Guidance control or influence the legal interpretation of the Agreement. In the 1999 Agreement there are a number of conditions to be met for which the claimant is responsible. These are examined in this chapter.

The 2008 Supplementary Uninsured Drivers' Agreement has now abolished the previous £300 excess on property damage and raised the limit for property damage to £1 million. Clauses 16(2), (3) and (4) of the 1999 Agreement are now amended. In addition, the MIB have published on its website a Memorandum of Understanding that enables the excess to be recovered in relation to accidents taking place between 11 June 2007 and 7 November 2008.

When the 1999 Uninsured Drivers' Agreement was first introduced, it provoked much criticism, which continues to this day. It also led to the accolade of 'Men in Black' being given to the Bureau. In December 1999, the Motor Accident Solicitors Society (MASS) issued judicial review proceedings against the government claiming that the new 1999 Agreement did not give effect to the European Motor Insurance Directives and, moreover, that it placed the innocent claimant at a disadvantage. The case came before the High Court in mid-2000 and was adjourned pending the hearing of *White* v. *White* [2001] UKHL 9. The parties then met to agree an amendment to the Notes for Guidance to the 1999 Agreement as the Bureau stated that it could not change the text of the actual Agreement. Eventually, in April

2002, MASS agreed to discontinue its judicial proceedings on the understanding that a new Revised Notes for Guidance would apply to all accidents occurring on or after 15 April 2002. As stated above, the legal effect of the Notes for Guidance on the 1999 Agreement is uncertain. Consequently, practitioners are advised to comply with the terms of the Agreement rather than the Revised Notes for Guidance.

The Bureau continues to maintain that the operation of the 1999 Agreement has not caused any difficulty. Certainly the vast majority of the cases that concern the 1999 Agreement relate to its conflict with European Motor Insurance Directives, and there is very little in the way of case law that relates to any practitioner falling foul of the Agreement on the grounds of non-compliance. Moreover, the decision of the House of Lords in *Horton* v. *Sadler and another* [2006] UKHL 27 (see **Chapter 6**) has opened up the possibility of re-issuing proceedings against an uninsured driver after the expiry of limitation, in circumstances where there has been a breach of the 1999 Agreement.

Nonetheless, the position whereby there is now an Agreement with Revised Notes for Guidance, a Supplementary Agreement and a Memorandum of Understanding creates difficulties for practitioners. These alterations and recent cases (see **Chapter 6**) have brought to light a number of legal and practical flaws in the 1999 Agreement and it remains a minefield for the unwary. Practitioners are strongly advised when handling such claims to make themselves familiar with the relevant Agreements and guidance. Practitioners should also regularly check the 'Downloadable Documents' section of the MIB's website for any new Agreements or Memoranda. As stated in **Chapter 1**, failure to read and follow the precise terms of these documents is a common cause of professional negligence claims.

2.2 THE UNINSURED DRIVER

A man is knocked down by a car and is injured. The driver of the car ought to have been insured under the Road Traffic Act 1988 (RTA 1988) against liability for such a claim. The driver is not so insured. He happens to be a 'man of straw', making it pointless to seek compensation from him personally. This was the first problem tackled by the Motor Insurers' Bureau. Clause 5 of the current Motor Insurers' Bureau Agreement relating to uninsured driver claims covers this type of case. It provides that, if the victim successfully brings proceedings against the uninsured driver, the Bureau will pay the amount of any 'unsatisfied judgment'.

The practice of the Bureau in cases where there is an insurance policy in existence is for the *insurers* concerned to deal with the claim. This is so even where the claim does not fall within the terms of the policy – for example, where a car was being used for a purpose other than one for which it was insured, e.g. business user when only insured for social use (see **Chapter 5**).

2.3   CLAUSES 1 TO 5 OF THE 1999 AGREEMENT

Clause 1 of the 1999 Agreement defines certain terms, such as 'relevant liability' which is the kind of liability that a motorist would be required to insure against under Part VI of RTA 1988. Clause 2 is entitled 'Meaning of references'. Clauses 2(2) and (3) tell the reader how to calculate time limits under the 1999 Agreement. In particular, clause 2(3) states that when the time limit in question is seven days or less, Saturday, Sunday, a bank holiday, Christmas Day or Good Friday shall be excluded. That is particularly useful when giving the Bureau notice of service of proceedings under clause 10 of the 1999 Agreement. However, practitioners should be aware that the time limits required by the Bureau for giving notice are quite tight. Consequently it is unwise to try and issue proceedings at a time when the court offices are closed (for instance over Christmas). Clause 2(5)(a) states that where the 1999 Agreement refers to any action that needs to be taken, that action may be taken by either the claimant or his or her solicitor. Clause 2(5)(b) states that where there is a requirement to give notice to, or to serve documents upon, the MIB or an insurer, that requirement shall be satisfied by the giving of the notice to a solicitor acting on behalf of the MIB or the insurer. Consequently, where the MIB appoints a solicitor on its behalf, it is quite permissible to serve the notices required under the 1999 Agreement on that solicitor.

Practitioners may wonder why the 1999 Agreement refers to an 'insurer' when the paying party will generally be the Bureau itself. Such an insurer would be an insurer by reason of art.75 of the Articles of Association of the MIB, otherwise known as a Domestic Regulation Insurer. Such an insurer can require a claimant to follow the 1999 Agreement (see **Chapter 5**).

Clause 3 states that where a solicitor or other representative of a claimant is involved, any decision or act done to, or by, such representative or payment to him or her is treated as if done to, or by, or paid to, a claimant of full age and capacity. Again, it seems that this clause has been inserted to protect the Bureau from claims similar to those it has had in the past of 'rogue' representatives who have not accounted fully (or, in some cases, at all) to the claimant.

However, clause 3 has other potential effects. It appears to mean that the MIB's decisions in relation to children or protected parties are to be treated as if they were made concerning adults of full capacity. In other words, none of the requirements concerning such parties contained in the Civil Procedure Rules 1998, SI 1998/3132, apply to the 1999 Agreement. In practice, the MIB submits to the jurisdiction of the court when dealing with these classes of person. It was also thought that clause 3 overrode the normal limitation rules. Paragraph 2.3 of the Revised Notes for Guidance makes it clear that the limitation period for personal injury claims by claimants not of full capacity is three years from the date of reaching age or capacity, and normal limitation rules will apply.

Clause 4 states that the 1999 Agreement comes into effect on 1 October 1999 and that the Agreement may be determined by the government and the MIB on giving 12 months' notice.

Clause 5 sets out the circumstances where the Bureau will pay compensation. Subject to the exceptions set out in **2.4** below, the Bureau will pay any amount outstanding under a judgment obtained by a victim claiming against an uninsured driver. The payment will include fixed or assessed costs. It will also include interest on the judgment debt (i.e. statutory interest, which varies; at present it is 8 per cent). If the claim includes a sum for items for which the Bureau is not liable, the amount of the costs will be reduced by the appropriate proportion.

It should be noted that there is nothing in the Agreement that affects the position at law of the parties to an action for damages arising out of the driving of a motor vehicle. The claimant must successfully establish his or her case against the person (or persons, if more than one) responsible for the accident in the usual way and must proceed to, and obtain, judgment. It should be noted that the issue of proceedings alone is insufficient to bring the claim within the terms of the 1999 Agreement.

The wording of clause 5 means that the Bureau will not pay any claim relating to an accident caused by a hit-and-run (untraced) driver (see **Chapter 3**) under the 1999 Agreement. This is because the Bureau requires a judgment to be entered against 'any person' and in the case of an untraced driver, no such person can be sued. Paragraph 11.1 of the Revised Notes for Guidance provides advice on what to do if it is unclear whether the driver is untraced or not.

In practice, it is not necessary to issue proceedings against every uninsured driver simply to obtain a judgment. The claimant is permitted to accept compensation under a settlement negotiated on his or her behalf with a person or persons responsible, or with the Bureau. The vast majority of claims are in fact settled by negotiation with the Bureau. Nevertheless, it is important to establish, at an early stage, the identity and the whereabouts of an uninsured driver, in case it later transpires that the driver is in fact untraced (see **Chapter 6**) and in all claims on the Bureau, it is highly recommended that proceedings are issued well before the limitation period expires.

2.4 THE EXCEPTIONS

The main exceptions are set out in clauses 6(1)(a) to (e) and are summarised below:

(a)   Where the claim arises out of the use of a vehicle owned by the Crown, unless someone had undertaken the responsibility for insuring that vehicle, or it was in fact insured. Clause 6(5)(a) says that where a vehicle is stolen from the Crown, it is deemed to continue in the Crown's possession while it is kept so removed. This clause appears to mean that even if a Crown vehicle is stolen, it remains the Crown's responsibility and potentially its liability while it is in the hands of a thief.

(b)   Where the claim arises out of the use of a vehicle which is not required to be insured, there is no liability to insure (under Part VI of RTA 1988), which would include vehicles listed under RTA 1988, s.144 (as amended). These include vehicles owned by the health service, a local authority, police vehicles or salvage vehicles. Another example would be where the vehicle was not being used on a 'road or other public place' and therefore pursuant to s.143(1)(a) would not be required to be insured. See **Chapter 5** for a discussion on vehicles that are not required to be insured.

(c)   A 'subrogated' claim, i.e. one made for the benefit of another person, e.g. arising under a motorist's comprehensive insurance policy or a credit hire agreement. Paragraph 3.4 of the Revised Notes for Guidance makes it clear that this clause is not intended to exclude claims for the gratuitous provision of care or travel and other miscellaneous expenses.

Clause 6(1)(c) and (later in the 1999 Agreement) clause 17 arguably cover a wide area of subrogated claims and other losses covered by insurance, including private hospital treatment and legal expenses cover. At present, the MIB do not appear to be refusing to pay costs where the claimant has had the benefit of legal representation.

There is also an argument that clause 6(1)(c) does not accord with the Second Motor Insurance Directive. In *McCall* v. *Poulton and another; Helphire (UK) Ltd and another intervening* [2008] EWCA Civ 1313, the claimant hired a replacement car from Helphire (UK) Ltd. He was also provided with an insurance policy issued by Angel Assistance Ltd. This provided post-accident cover for the claimant's legal costs and Helphire's charges in the event that they were not recovered from the defendant who turned out to be uninsured. The claimant made a claim on his Angel policy, which was paid. He then sued the defendant and the MIB, who compensated him for his injury and his other losses but refused to compensate for the hire charges, relying on clauses 6(1)(c) and 17(1) of the 1999 Uninsured Drivers' Agreement. The claimant argued before the Court of Appeal that the wording of art.1.4 of the Second Motor Insurance Directive included a claim for car hire. The 1999 Agreement was a contract made for the purposes of discharging the UK's obligations under that Directive. Reference was made to *Marleasing SA* v. *La Comercial Internacional de Alimentacion SA* (Case C-106/89) [1990] ECRI-4135 where the European Court of Justice had said that, in applying national law, national courts should interpret national law, so far as possible, in the light of the wording and the purpose of a Directive in order to achieve the result targeted by that Directive. In addition, it was argued that the claimant could rely on the Directive, as it was directly effected. One of the conditions for direct effect was that the MIB should be regarded as an 'emanation of the State'. The Court of Appeal said that guidance from the European Court of Justice was required. The issues were:

- whether the *Marleasing* doctrine applied to the MIB Agreements;
- whether the MIB was an emanation of the State.

The answer to these issues holds the key to the liability of the MIB, which would affect other cases. Therefore, these questions were referred to the European Court of Justice. At present, its judgment is awaited.

In the meantime, the Court of Appeal has recently ruled on the issue of whether an insurer can recover its subrogated loss against an insurer caught by RTA 1988, s.151(2)(a). In the case of *Bristol Alliance Limited Partnership* v. *Williams* [2011] EWHC 1657 (QB) the court initially held that a claimant's insurer was entitled to recover against a defendant's insurer, even though the damage was the result of a deliberate act by the defendant insured as part of his attempt to commit suicide. However, the Court of Appeal reversed this decision in *EUI Ltd* v. *Bristol Alliance Partnership Ltd* [2012] EWCA Civ 1267. Section 151 gave no right of recovery against the defendant's insurer, because the terms of the policy expressly excluded damage caused by the original act of the driver. A claim might be made in these circumstances to the MIB, but its Agreement did not extend to compensating anyone who had suffered property damage, where such damage was already insured by the victim's own insurer. This decision would, of course, mean that the claimant's credit hire insurers in *McCall* could not recover their loss, but as stated above, the decision of the ECJ is still awaited in that case.

(d) A claim for damage to a motor vehicle or losses arising therefrom where that vehicle was uninsured, and the owner knew, or should have known, that the vehicle was uninsured. Essentially, this clause prevents the uninsured motorist (who is the blameless victim of another uninsured motorist) from pursuing his or her own property damage claim against the MIB.

(e) Any claim by a passenger who knew, or could be taken to have known, that the vehicle was uninsured, or had been stolen or used for a crime. See the House of Lords' judgment in *White* v. *White* [2001] UKHL 9, which sets out the criteria for decisions on 'knowledge' (see **Chapter 6**).

Clause 6(1)(e) is then followed by three sub-clauses (2), (3) and (4) which further define the exceptions in clause 6(1)(e). Clause 6(2) states that the liability referred to in clause 6(1)(e) is a liability incurred by the owner or registered keeper or a person using the vehicle in which the claimant was being carried. This means that it is not only the person who drives an uninsured vehicle who can be sued, but also the person who owns the vehicle if he or she permits someone else to drive it.

Under clause 6(3) the burden of proving the matters in clause 6(1)(e) (i.e. the absence or inadequacy of insurance cover) falls on the MIB. There then follows a number of circumstances where knowledge will be presumed. These include the fact that the claimant was the owner or the registered keeper of the vehicle. Thus, according to the MIB Agreement, a person who is injured in his or her own uninsured vehicle will be deemed to know that there was no insurance.

Finally, clause 6(4) states that the claimant's knowledge cannot be affected by self-induced drink or drugs. Thus, according to the MIB Agreement, a claimant cannot rely on the excuse of being drunk to argue that he or she did not know that the vehicle was uninsured.

Practitioners need to be aware that the House of Lords' judgment in *White* v. *White* [2001] UKHL 9 severely restricts the Bureau's interpretation of the concept of 'knowledge' as set out in the 1999 Agreement. The way in which clause 6(1)(e) and its subsequent clauses should apply as a matter of law is discussed in more detail in **Chapter 6**. Furthermore, *Candolin* v. *Vahinkovakuutusosakeyhtio Pohjola* (Case C-537/03) [2006] RTR 1 (which deals with the effect of drink on a person's knowledge and which is discussed in **Chapter 5**) also restricts the effect of clause 6(4).

Further exceptions are set out in clause 15 of the 1999 Agreement. The Bureau will not pay any claim where the claimant has not assigned to the Bureau or its nominee the unsatisfied judgment, including costs. The Bureau has a department that makes a limited recovery from uninsured drivers each year, hence the importance of this clause. The claimant must also undertake to repay to the Bureau any sums received under a judgment that has been set aside, and any sums received from other sources under the judgment. In other words, claimants must not be allowed to benefit from a duplication of their compensation.

Clause 17 allows the Bureau to deduct any sum a claimant has received from the Policyholders Protection Board (now the Financial Services Authority), an insurer under an insurance agreement or any other source, such as a defendant with means or the Criminal Injuries Compensation Authority. Again, the purpose of this clause is to prevent duplication of damages, but, as has been seen above, it is not clear how this clause should operate in light of the Court of Appeal's decision in *McCall* v. *Poulton* (see above).

2.5   APPLICATION FORMS AND THE CAPACITY OF CLAIMANT

The first step in making an application to the Bureau is to prepare a formal application using the form provided on the MIB website. Clause 7(1) of the 1999 Agreement gives the Bureau the right to refuse to accept an application if it is not in the correct form, if it does not give the correct information and if it is not accompanied by such documents as the Bureau may reasonably require. Great care must be taken in the completion of the form, particularly if liability is likely to be in dispute.

Paragraph 5.1 of the Notes for Guidance provides for claimants who are not legally advised. If the claim is made within 14 days before the expiry of the limitation period, the Bureau requires the completed application form within 21 days after proceedings are issued.

Clause 7(2) allows the Bureau to refuse the application if it is not signed by the claimant or a solicitor acting on his or her behalf. It appears that this clause will only be invoked if the Bureau is not satisfied as to the status of the party signing the form and his or her relationship with the claimant, or it has any doubt that the claimant is fully aware of the contents and effect of the application.

It must be inferred from this provision that some representatives have been troublesome in the past in pursuing claims on behalf of claimants without acting in their best interests and without having the restraints imposed by a professional body (such as the Solicitors Regulation Authority). Clause 3 appears to echo this concern.

2.6 ISSUE OF PROCEEDINGS

Under para.5.3 of the Revised Notes for Guidance, the Bureau should be joined as a defendant unless there is good reason not to do so. It is difficult to think of any circumstances in which the Bureau would not be joined as an additional defendant once it has been decided to issue proceedings. The Notes also set out the precise wording to be used in the Particulars of Claim for suing the Bureau, including an application for a declaration of the Bureau's contingent liability to satisfy any judgment entered against the uninsured driver.

The Revised Notes for Guidance state that in these circumstances (i.e. when the Bureau is added as a defendant, 'the Court will advise the relevant events direct'. The 'relevant events' comprise the notices that are required to be given to the Bureau under clauses 9(3), 11 and 12 of the 1999 MIB Agreement. Practitioners are advised to treat that statement with caution in the light of potential delays on the part of the court and other factors that may delay an otherwise timely notice. It is better to give notice as required by those clauses in any event.

Practitioners are strongly advised not to leave the issue of proceedings in a MIB case until the last moment, since this is another potential area for professional negligence claims. The main reason is that if the MIB raises some non-compliance point under clauses 8 to 12 (which we consider below), it is possible to re-issue proceedings and start again. Obviously the cost of the initial proceedings may be lost but it is suggested that the MIB is far less likely to raise a non-compliance point if it knows that the claimant can re-issue proceedings.

The other reason for issuing early is that the MIB may not make any enquiries into the whereabouts of the defendant until after proceedings are issued and served. It is at this point that it may conclude that the defendant is untraced. If that is the case, the claimant may find that he or she has fallen outside the time limits stipulated in the 2003 Untraced Drivers' Agreement.

It is possible to issue proceedings in an uninsured case outside the limitation period (see *Horton* v. *Sadler and another* [2006] UKHL 27 and other cases in **Chapter 6**). However, the claimant has still to persuade the court that limitation should not apply so as to bar the claim.

Practitioners should also consider carefully whom they should be suing. Clause 14 requires the claimant to take all reasonable steps to obtain judgment against any other defendants who may be liable, although the MIB should grant the claimant an indemnity for taking this action. It may be that a highway authority is liable for failing to maintain the road, or there may be some doubt about the identity of a joyrider where there are multiple persons in the defendant's car, each of whom deny that they were behind the wheel at the time of the accident. As we will see in **Chapter 6**, there are certain circumstances where both passengers and driver may each have to share liability for the accident, or it may be the owner of the vehicle who has to pick up the final bill. The case of *Barnard* v. *Sully* (1931) 47 TLR 557 demonstrates this last point. The court held that there was a presumption that the owner of a car was the driver at the time of the accident, or that the person driving the car was that driver's servant or agent. There are cases where registered keepers have abandoned their uninsured cars following an accident in an attempt to evade prosecution, and then claimed that they had sold the vehicle to an unknown person prior to that accident. Alternatively, the owner of the uninsured vehicle may have allowed someone else to drive the vehicle, but subsequently claims that the vehicle was taken without his or her knowledge or authority.

2.7 CLAUSES 8 TO 12 OF THE 1999 AGREEMENT

These clauses set out precisely what the claimant must do when issuing proceedings and the procedural steps required by the Civil Procedure Rules 1998. Any failure to comply with these clauses may lead to the MIB refusing to pay the claim.

2.7.1 Clause 8 – Services of notices

Practitioners should first have regard to clause 8, which deals with service of notices. This states that any notice required to be given or document to be supplied to the MIB pursuant to clauses 9 to 12 can only be sent by facsimile transmission or by registered (now special) or recorded delivery. In para.5.6 of the Revised Notes for Guidance, the MIB says that it will accept service by DX, first class post, personal service or any other form of service allowed by the Civil Procedure Rules 1998. Service by fax may not be practical if the documents to be sent are bulky (although the authors have encountered practitioners who use this method regularly). Recorded delivery or delivery by courier is possibly the safest way to effect service, followed up by a telephone call to the MIB, which records receipt of all post. It is important to realise that there is no deemed service of a document on the MIB. A practitioner has to be sure that the document has arrived, otherwise there is potential non-compliance with the 1999 MIB Agreement.

2.7.2 Clause 9 – Obligation to give notice of issue of proceedings

The claimant has 14 days in which to give the MIB notice in writing that he or she has commenced legal proceedings. Clause 9(1) states that 'proper notice' of the bringing of proceedings must be given:

(a) in the case of proceedings in respect of a relevant liability which is covered by a contract of insurance with an insurer whose identity can be ascertained, to that insurer;

(b) in any other case, to the MIB.

Clause 9(2) lists the information and documentation that must be supplied at that point:

(a) notice in writing that proceedings have been issued by claim form, writ or other means;

(b) a copy of the sealed claim form, writ or other official document providing evidence of the commencement of the proceedings;

(c) a copy or details of any insurance policy providing benefits in the case of the death, bodily injury or damage to property to which the proceedings relate where the claimant is the insured party and the benefits are available to him or her – the original application form to the MIB actually requests this information;

(d) copies of all correspondence in the possession of the claimant or (as the case may be) his or her solicitor or agent to or from the defendant, his or her solicitor, insurers or agent relevant to:

  (i) the death, bodily injury or damage for which the defendant is alleged to be responsible; or

  (ii) any contract of insurance which covers, or which may or has been alleged to cover, liability for such death, injury or damage the benefit of which is, or is claimed to be, available to the defendant;

(e) a copy of the particulars of claim whether served or not;

(f) a copy of all other documents which are required under the appropriate rules of procedure to be served on the defendant with the claim form, writ, or other originating process or with the particulars of claim, i.e. notice of issue of legal aid, certificate of suitability;

(g) such other information about the relevant proceedings as the MIB may reasonably specify.

Clause 9(3) states that if, in the case of proceedings commenced in England and Wales, the particulars of claim (including any document to be served therewith) has not yet been served with the claim form or other originating process, clause 9(2)(e) shall be sufficiently complied with if a copy thereof is served on the MIB not later than seven days after it is served on the defendant. Practitioners are advised to serve all the issued documents together, rather than fall foul of a missed time limit.

2.7.3 Clause 10 – Obligation to give notice of service of proceedings

The claimant must give notice of service of the proceedings to the MIB in writing. The notice must be given (clause 10(3)):

(a)   seven days after:

    (i)   the date when the claimant receives notification from the Court that service of the Claim Form or other originating process has occurred,

    (ii)   the date when the claimant receives notification from the Defendant that service of the Claim Form or other originating process has occurred, or

    (iii) the date of personal service, or

(b)   fourteen days after the date when service is deemed to have occurred in accordance with the Civil Procedure Rules,

whichever of those days occurs first.

The Revised Notes for Guidance state that the MIB will accept the notice of service of the claim form within 14 days of deemed or personal service (para.6.4).

2.7.4   Clause 11 – Obligation to give further information

The MIB is not liable unless the claimant within seven days of any of the following events, gives notice to the MIB of:

(a)   the filing of a defence in the relevant proceedings;

(b)   any amendment of the particulars of claim or any amendment of, or addition to, the schedule or other document required to be served therewith; and

(c)   either:

    (i)   the setting down of the case for trial; or

    (ii)   where the court gives notice in writing of the date of the trial date, the date when the notice is received.

In the case of a filing of a defence, particulars of claim or any amendment of, or addition to, any schedule or other document required to be served therewith, a copy thereof must also be supplied to the MIB.

Clause 11(2) gives the MIB the right to ask for further information as it may reasonably require.

The Revised Notes for Guidance, again, give a concession on the notice given to the MIB. The seven-day period referred to in clause 11(1) is extended to 14 days (para.7.2).

2.7.5   Clause 12 – Obligation to give notice of applying for judgment

This clause states that the MIB shall incur no liability unless the claimant has, after commencement of proceedings, and not less than 35 days before the appropriate date, given notice in writing of his or her intention to apply for judgment. The appropriate date means the date when the application for judgment is made or, as the case may be, the signing of judgment occurs. The Revised Notes for Guidance state that the 35 days' notice does not apply where the court enters judgment of its own motion (para.7.4).

2.8 ASCERTAINING THE IDENTITY OF THE DEFENDANT AND WHETHER INSURED

It is for the claimant to make reasonable enquiries to establish the existence of insurance cover of the vehicle causing the injury or damage. Generally, the MID (see **1.5**) will reveal whether the defendant is insured or not, but that information is not conclusive. Furthermore, while the police are well equipped to apprehend and prosecute uninsured drivers, some defendants do manage to dodge the long arm of the law.

Clause 13(a) of the 1999 Agreement stipulates that the claimant must 'as soon as reasonably practicable' after the accident, exercise his or her statutory right under RTA 1988, s.154(1) (i.e. make a request for insurance details). If the MID reported that a vehicle was uninsured, that would trigger clause 13. The MIB will have a record of the date of the claimant's request for information, and any delay in compliance with clause 13 could prove problematic later on.

All reasonable efforts have to be made to obtain the name and address of the registered keeper of the vehicle. Paragraph 4.2 of the Revised Notes for Guidance sets out the minimum steps that should be taken. If there is no reply to a letter sent by special delivery and all other attempts to contact the defendant have failed, then the claimant must submit a formal report to the police (clause 13(b)). The claimant may also be required to authorise the Bureau to make further enquiries on his or her behalf, presumably at the expense of the Bureau.

Paragraph 4.1 of the Revised Notes for Guidance states that the claimant is accepted by the Bureau to have complied with clause 13(a) by completing and signing the Bureau's application form. Nevertheless, a prudent claimant (or a cautious legal adviser) would be expected to take the minimum steps set out in para.4.2. It is recommended that the claimant should send a letter by special delivery to the defendant and, on its return, make a formal complaint to the police and obtain a crime number from them. If the defendant has been prosecuted, no formal report is required but cases do arise where there has been no police involvement with, or criminal prosecution of, the uninsured defendant. In such circumstances it is considered prudent to instruct an enquiry agent to endeavour to locate the defendant.

Practitioners should take great care over this clause. In an unreported case, *Shapoor* v. *Promo Designs* (unreported, Romford County Court, 1 May 2009), the MIB took the point (ultimately unsuccessfully) that the claimant had not complied properly with clause 13 of the 1999 Agreement.

In any event, the establishment of the defendant's identity early on in an uninsured driver claim may serve to avoid any later attempt by the Bureau to refer the claimant to the less generous 2003 Untraced Drivers' Agreement. Paragraphs 4.3 and 4.4 of the Revised Notes for Guidance set out what should be done if an insurer is located or if it transpires that there is no insurer. Paragraph 11.2 of the Revised Notes for Guidance advises:

In those cases where it is unclear whether the owner or driver of a vehicle has been correctly identified it is sensible for the claimant to register a claim under both this Agreement and the Untraced Drivers' Agreement following which MIB will advise which Agreement will, in its view, apply in the circumstances of the particular case.

2.9 SUING ALL LIABLE PARTIES

Clause 14(a) states that the MIB shall incur no liability unless the claimant has (if so required) taken all reasonable steps to obtain judgment against every person who may be liable for the accident. This clause enables the Bureau to require a claimant to bring in another party, who may be insured and therefore who may also be able to satisfy the judgment rather than the burden falling on the uninsured driver and, ultimately, the Bureau. The sub-clause does say that in these circumstances, the Bureau will indemnify the claimant against the possibility of losing the case against that other party. This is a useful provision in a road traffic accident where there is more than one defendant and it is unclear where liability will ultimately fall.

Clause 14(b) enables the Bureau to require the claimant to join it into proceedings, although, as we have seen above, the Bureau should be joined as a defendant unless there is good reason not to do so.

2.10 THE POSITION AFTER JUDGMENT AND PROPERTY DAMAGE

Although the Bureau is obliged to make payment under a judgment not satisfied within seven days, such judgment may be set aside (or appealed successfully) and with it the Bureau's obligation to pay. The Bureau must notify a claimant as soon as possible if it decides not to satisfy a judgment. Where a judgment is set aside, the claimant is required to repay any sums received from the Bureau (clause 15(b)).

The Bureau is only obliged to make payment under a judgment if the claimant has assigned that judgment to the Bureau or its nominee (clause 15(a)). Although it may be thought that all uninsured drivers are 'men of straw', the MIB do have a department that seeks to recover money from the original tortfeasor. In its 2010 Annual Report, the MIB reported that it had recovered £4.77 million from uninsured drivers.

There will be an apportionment of the sum recovered between the items for which the Bureau is, and is not, liable (clause 21).

Clause 16 provides for the payment by the Bureau for damage to property. The 2008 Supplementary Uninsured Drivers' Agreement abolished the previous £300 excess for property damage and raised the limit for property damage to £1 million.

2.11 THE REASONED RESPONSE AND REFERRAL TO THE SECRETARY OF STATE

Under clause 18 of the current Agreement, where notice has been given to the Bureau pursuant to clause 9(1) and (2), the Bureau is under an obligation to provide a reasonable reply as soon as reasonably practicable to the claimant as to whether it is going to meet the claim. This clause may be useful to encourage the Bureau to make its position clear and to waive any remaining difficult requirements under the Agreement.

Clause 19 enables the MIB to refer any dispute as to the reasonableness of a requirement which it may have made for the supply of information or the taking of any step by the claimant to the Secretary of State, whose decision shall be final. The authors are not aware of any such case. In practice, disputes over the meaning and operation of the 1999 Agreement are dealt with by the court, as will be seen in **Chapter 6**.

2.12 RECOVERIES AND APPORTIONMENTS

Clause 20 provides for the situation where an Article 75 Insurer (see **Chapter 5**) pays out to a victim of an uninsured driver in relation to an accident caused by its own 'insured'. In such a situation, the 1999 Agreement does not prevent the insurer (or the MIB for that matter) from making a recovery from the blameworthy motorist.

Clause 21 covers the situation where the MIB has been assigned an unsatisfied judgment by a claimant, and proceeds to make a partial recovery against a blameworthy uninsured driver. The MIB is allowed to apportion the sum that it recovers from that driver between any liability covered by the 1999 Agreement and any other liability that is not. It will then account to the claimant for any monies that it receives relating to the liability not covered by the 1999 Agreement, and keep the monies it has already paid out to the same claimant for the liability that is covered by the Agreement.

Clause 22 allows the MIB to carry out its functions by the use of agents. Nowadays the Bureau prefers to deal with all claims in-house, although it will appoint solicitors from its own panel to handle issued claims.

2.13 INTERIM PAYMENTS

Under rule 25.7 of the Civil Procedure Rules 1998 the court can order an interim payment to be made by a defendant to a claimant. Rule 25.7(1)(e) provides for the situation where there are two or more defendants and an order for an interim payment is sought against either defendant. Under rule 25.7(1)(e)(ii), a defendant can include one whose liability would be met by an insurer under RTA 1988, s.151

or an insurer acting under the Motor Insurers' Bureau Agreement, or the MIB where it is acting for itself. This puts claims under the 1999 Uninsured Drivers' Agreement firmly under the scope of rule 25.7 of the Civil Procedure Rules. Paragraph 8 of the Revised Notes for Guidance confirms this position.

2.14 'CLAWBACK' PROVISIONS

It should be noted that the Social Security (Recovery of Benefits) Act 1997 and the regulations made under it apply equally to the MIB as they do to any other defendant. They provide for recovery (i.e. 'clawback') of benefits when compensation is paid by the MIB on claims arising out of accidents caused by uninsured drivers. Section 1(1) of the Act applies to any person who makes a payment (whether on his or her own behalf or not) to, or in respect of, any other person in consequence of any accident, injury or disease suffered by the other, and s.1(2) states that such a payment can be 'in pursuance of a compensation scheme for motor accidents'.

2.15 CHECK LIST FOR UNINSURED MOTORIST CLAIMS

The following check list may assist practitioners when investigating whether a claim is likely to succeed:

1. Consider evidence to show that the claimant's injury was caused by a motor vehicle.
2. Consider evidence that the accident took place on a road or other public place.
3. Is the application excluded under any of the exclusion provisions in the 1999 Agreement?
4. Is the claimant caught by any of the issues discussed in **Chapter 6**? For instance, did the claimant get into the negligent driver's car knowing that there was no insurance, or was the claimant 'using' the vehicle?
5. Has the claimant reported the incident to the police and is there a police report? (See clause 13 of the 1999 Agreement.)
6. Have all reasonable enquiries been made to trace the driver? If there is doubt about identifying the driver, should there be a parallel claim under the 2003 Untraced Drivers' Agreement? (See **Chapter 6**.)
7. Have all reasonable enquiries been made to ascertain the driver's insurance status?
8. Were there any other parties involved? If so, were they insured? Consider whether their drivers should also be sued and ask the Bureau for an indemnity. (See clause 14 of the 1999 Agreement.)
9. Does the evidence suggest a deliberate or concerted act by the driver to run down the victim? In such cases, the possibility of a parallel claim under the

Criminal Injuries Compensation Scheme should be considered, but see **Chapter 6** for a discussion of this issue.

10.   Should a diary note be made to issue proceedings well before limitation, so as to avoid the possibility of having to re-issue after limitation because of non-compliance with the provisions of the 1999 Agreement?

CHAPTER 3

The 'hit-and-run' motorist (the Untraced Drivers' Agreement)

3.1 INTRODUCTION

Section 170 of RTA 1988 requires a driver to stop following an accident, and, if required to do so, give his or her name and address as well as the name and address of the owner of the vehicle. Where there has been a personal injury, the driver must also produce his or her insurance details to the police or some person 'having reasonable grounds.' If the driver does not do so, he or she must report the accident to the police and produce his or her insurance details.

Most law-abiding drivers will stop after an accident and exchange details with any other party. Alternatively, the police will attend, at which point details will be taken and insurance checked. However, in former times, there were many who gave false particulars, had false number plates and who disappeared before, or even after, the summons was heard in the magistrates' court. The scope for such criminal activity has lessened since the introduction of the MID and the ability of the police not only to check a driver's insurance details on the spot, but also to seize the vehicle to prevent it being driven away. Consequently, an uninsured driver or a driver without valid insurance may be tempted simply to drive away or otherwise flee the scene before that driver and his or her vehicle are identified.

Not unlike compulsive drinkers who continue their drinking habits after medical advice, or who have a record of drunk and disorderly convictions, there are 'compulsive drivers'. These are not unknown to advocates who have to cobble together some weak, but otherwise impassioned, plea, by way of mitigation on *further* driving offences after disqualification (or disqualifications).

Many of the more serious accidents dealt with by the MIB involve untraced drivers, particularly joyriders. Victims of these unidentified criminals' behaviour would have no redress were it not for the provisions for payment by the MIB.

Under the original 1946 Agreement, the Bureau was under no *liability* to pay compensation to the victims in untraced motorist cases. It was obliged only to give 'sympathetic consideration' to claims made by the victim where it was satisfied that a motor vehicle was involved, and, apart from the vehicle owner or driver not being traced, a claim would lie in law. In many such cases, after giving 'sympathetic consideration' to the facts and the injuries, the Bureau made an *ex gratia* payment to the victim or, where the victim had died, to dependants. 'Sympathetic considera-tion' was all that was required under the 1946 Agreement. The Bureau thus had what amounted to a complete discretion whether or not to make a payment, and as to the amount of the payment. Later Agreements have introduced an *obligation* to deal with claims of this kind.

The 1969 Agreement extended the obligations of the Bureau to include untraced motorist claims. It applied to accidents that occurred on or after 1 May 1969 but before 1 December 1972. The 1972 Agreement applied to accidents that occurred on or after 1 December 1972. The 1996 Agreement applied to accidents on or after 1 July 1996.

The 2003 Agreement applies to accidents on or after 14 February 2003 and is the current Agreement. It was supplemented by the Supplementary Untraced Drivers' Agreement 2008, which came into force on 1 February 2009 and applied to accidents occurring after midnight from that date onwards. There is a second Supplementary Agreement dated 15 April 2011 which came into force from that date. Finally there is a Memorandum of Understanding published by the MIB on its website which deals with the effect of *Byrne (a Minor)* v. *The Motor Insurers' Bureau and the Secretary of State for Transport* [2008] EWCA Civ 574 (see **3.3** below).

As with the 1999 Uninsured Drivers' Agreement, practitioners are strongly advised, when handling these claims, to make themselves familiar with the *precise* terms of the 2003 Agreement, its Supplementary Agreements and the Memoran-dum of Understanding. Practitioners should also regularly check the 'Download-able Documents' section of the MIB's website for any new Agreements or Memoranda. Failure to read and follow the precise terms of these documents is a common cause of claims failing or being prejudiced in some way.

3.2 THE UNTRACED DRIVER

Clause 1 of the 2003 Agreement (the interpretation clause) uses the term 'unidenti-fied person' for an untraced driver. The distinction between an uninsured and an untraced/unidentified driver can be found in *Gurtner* v. *Circuit* [1968] 1 All ER 328 and *Clarke and another* v. *Vedel and another* [1979] RTR 26 which we discuss in **Chapter 6**. However, the crucial point for practitioners is that where where there is an untraced driver there is no defendant who can be sued and the Civil Procedure Rules 1998 will not be engaged. There is limited scope within the Agreement to take court action against the MIB under clause 32 of its own Agreement. It is also possible in certain limited circumstances to take the decision of a MIB appointed arbitrator to the Commercial Court. Furthermore, claimants have sued the MIB in untraced driver cases in conjunction with the government where the interpretation of a Motor Insurance Directive is at stake (see **Chapter 6**). Nonetheless, as was seen in *Persson* v. *London Country Buses* [1974] 1 WLR 569, a claimant cannot sue the

MIB direct. The proper course is to submit an application and follow the terms of the 2003 Agreement, as amended by the two Supplementary Agreements referred to at **3.1** above.

3.3   TERMS OF THE 2003 AGREEMENT

Clause 1 of the Agreement begins with a set of definitions. The forerunner to the 2003 Agreement contained a clause 1(1)(e) to the effect that deliberate acts were excluded from the terms of the Untraced Drivers' Agreement. Consequently, any such claim would have to be submitted to the Criminal Injuries Compensation Authority (CICA). This clause has been removed and it is submitted that the MIB should deal with a claim involving an untraced driver even where the accident has arisen out of an intentional act (see **Chapter 6**). Practitioners are advised to make claims under both schemes, although obviously the compensation afforded under the 2003 Agreement is not as limited as that set out by the CICA in its 'tariff'.

Clause 2 is similar to clause 3 of the 1999 Uninsured Drivers' Agreement (see **Chapter 2**). It simply says that the MIB's decisions in relation to children or protected parties are to be treated as if they were made concerning adults. In other words, none of the requirements concerning such parties contained in the Civil Procedure Rules apply to the 2003 Agreement. Practitioners should remember that when handling a claim brought on behalf of a child or a protected person, there is no means of having any settlement approved by a judge because there are no court proceedings against any defendant. However, clause 25 (see below) of the 2003 Agreement does make some limited provision for this type of applicant.

Clause 3 sets out the commencement and duration of the Agreement.

Clause 4(1) specifies the main conditions to be satisfied for an applicant to make a successful claim under the Agreement. The Agreement applies where the death of, or bodily injury to, a person or damage to any property of a person has been caused by, or has arisen out of, the use of a motor vehicle on a road or other public place in Great Britain. Consequently, one cannot claim under the Agreement if one is struck by an untraced push bike or horse and cart since neither are motor vehicles!

Clause 4(1) specifies other conditions. The accident must have occurred on or after 14 February 2003 and in circumstances giving rise to liability of a kind required to be covered by an insurance policy. It must not be possible to identify the person responsible and the applicant must have made an application in writing to the MIB within the time limits set out in clause 4(3).

Clause 4(2) says that where an application is signed by someone else other than the applicant or his or her solicitors, the MIB may refuse to accept the application. This echoes clause 7(2) in the 1999 Agreement (see **Chapter 2**).

Clause 4(3) provides the time limits for making an application under the 2003 Agreement, as well as those for reporting the accident to the police, and other requirements.

Before the 2008 Supplementary Agreement, a three-year time limit was applied to claims involving personal injury (with a 15-year long stop) and a nine-month time limit for property claims (with a two-year long stop).

The time limits in this clause have been substantially amended by the 2008 and 2011 Supplementary Agreements, following *Byrne (a Minor)* v. *The Motor Insurers' Bureau and the Secretary of State for Transport* [2008] EWCA Civ 574 (see **Chapter 6**). This case determined that the rules contained in the Limitation Act 1980 should apply to the applicant (who was a child at the time of the accident) rather than the three-year time limit specified in what was then the 1972 Untraced Drivers' Agreement. The 2008 Supplementary Agreement imports the Limitation Act 1980 into the 2003 Agreement. This means that an applicant under the 2003 Agreement who is a child or a protected party is not bound by the previous Agreement limits for *personal injury claims*. In addition, the Memorandum of Understanding attached to the 2003 Agreement specifies how the MIB will deal with applications brought by persons who previously found themselves unable to claim before the decision in *Byrne*. As for *property claims*, clause 4(3)(a)(ii) of the 2003 Agreement remains. Thus property claims must be brought within nine months of the accident. The long stop periods for personal injury and property damage under clause 4(3)(b) were removed by the 2008 Supplementary Agreement.

In addition, practitioners also need to be aware of the additional time limits contained in clause 4(3)(c), (d) and (e) of the 2003 Agreement, which are very tight indeed. Non-compliance can prove fatal to the claim. Briefly, clause 4(3)(c) requires the applicant to report the accident to the police within 14 days in the case of personal injury, and within five days in the case of property damage, or where that is not reasonably possible, the accident must be reported as soon as reasonably possible. Clause 4(3)(d) requires the applicant to produce 'satisfactory evidence' of having made the report in clause 4(3)(e). Under clause 4(3)(e) the applicant must have co-operated with the police.

The police report (if there is one) forms a crucial part of the application, because the MIB will rely heavily on any such report to come to a determination. In addition, practitioners need to be aware of clause 9(1) which links the award of interest to the date on which the MIB receives the police report (see below). Clause 4(3)(c), (d) and (e) appear to discourage claims for minor injuries under the 2003 Agreement, where the applicant has simply not bothered to report the matter at all, but as far as the practitioner is concerned, these clauses leave very little scope for error.

A word of explanation is needed about the rather confusing changes made to the numbering of the 2003 Agreement by the 2008 and 2011 Supplementary Agreements. Clauses 4(3)(c), (d) and (e) were changed over to clause 4(3)(b), (c) and (d) by the 2008 Supplementary Agreement. Clause 4(3)(b) was specifically omitted. The 2011 Supplementary Agreement then changed clause 4(3)(b), (c) and (d) back to clauses 4(3)(c), (d) and (e). The authors assume that the effect is still to leave clause 4(3)(b) omitted by the 2008 Supplementary Agreement. Clause 4(3)(b) was the former clause in the 2003 Agreement that provided for a 15-year long stop period for making a personal injury claim and a two-year long stop period for a property damage claim. As stated above, these time limits were removed by the 2008 Supplementary Agreement following *Byrne*. Thus the original numbering of clause 4(3) of the 2003 Agreement remains the same with clause 4(3)(b) omitted.

Regardless of the relaxed time limits introduced by the 2008 Supplementary Agreement, practitioners are not advised to hold up submitting claims to the MIB under the 2003 Untraced Drivers' Agreement until a child reaches adulthood or a protected party obtains capacity. The nature of these claims means that evidence as to liability can often be scant and the passage of time can seriously prejudice any investigation. For this reason alone, applications for children and protected parties should be submitted *as soon as possible*. In addition, while clause 7 states that the MIB shall, at its own cost, take all reasonable steps to investigate the claim (and such reasonable steps would include obtaining the police report), it cannot be assumed that it will pursue as thorough an investigation as that of the applicant's solicitors. For that reason, particularly in a large claim, obtaining relevant evidence should not be left to the MIB. The processing of a claim can be delayed by (for instance) problems in obtaining the police report or it may be that no police report is prepared at all. In the meantime, crucial witnesses may disappear and memories of the accident may fade.

Clause 5(1) makes several exclusions, which we paraphrase here. The text of the agreement is more detailed, but practitioners will note that exceptions relied on by the MIB under the 2003 Agreement are very similar to those found under clause 6(1)(a) to (e) in the 1999 Agreement, and, consequently, the same considerations that are discussed in **Chapter 2** will apply.

(a)   Clause 5(1)(a) has been amended by the 2011 Supplementary Agreement.

By contrast with the 1999 Uninsured Drivers' Agreement, where the excess was abolished by the 2008 Supplementary Uninsured Drivers' Agreement, the MIB is not required to pay the first £300, the 'specified excess' in an untraced driver claim. However, the position on claiming for property damage has been changed by the 2011 Supplementary Agreement. Previously, under clause 5(1)(a), the applicant was not allowed to make a claim for *property damage only* caused by an unidentified vehicle. Clause 5(3) stated that where a claim was made for both personal injury and property damage, the 2003 Agreement would not apply to the property damage claim.

Now, under the new clause 5(1)(a), the applicant may make a claim for property damage, but only if the MIB has paid a claim for 'significant personal injury' either to the applicant or some other applicant arising out of the same accident. The 2011 Supplementary Agreement defines precisely what is meant by 'significant personal injury'. Very briefly, it is an injury that results in death or four or more days of consecutive hospital treatment commencing within 30 days of the accident. The problem with the former version of clause 5(1)(a) (and also clause 5(3)) was that the Fifth Motor Insurance Directive restricted the right of the MIB to avoid paying out on claims for property damage. The Directive said that the option of limiting or excluding compensation on the basis that the vehicle was not identified should not apply where the MIB had paid compensation for significant personal injuries to any victim of the same accident. For this reason, the 2011 Supplementary Agreement introduced these changes to bring the 2003 Agreement in line with the Directive. Clause 5(3) has now been omitted by the 2011 Supplementary Agreement.

(b)   Where the accident was caused by a vehicle owned by, or in the possession of, the Crown.

(c)   Where the person suffering injury was voluntarily allowing himself or herself to be carried in the vehicle responsible, and before the commencement of his or her journey in the vehicle (or after such commencement if that person could reasonably be expected to have alighted from the vehicle), he or she knew, or ought to have known, that the vehicle:

   (i)   had been stolen or unlawfully taken;
   (ii)   was being used without insurance;
   (iii) was being used in the course of a crime;
   (iv)   was being used as a means of escape from, or avoidance of, lawful apprehension.

(d)   Where the injury was caused by terrorism.

(e)   Where the property damaged is insured.

(f)   Where the applicant's property, i.e. his or her vehicle, is damaged, and the applicant has no insurance for that vehicle.

(g)   Where the application is made by someone other than the person suffering injury or his or her personal representative, i.e. where a cause of action has been assigned to the applicant or the applicant is acting pursuant to a right of subrogation. Again, the effectiveness of this clause is subject to some doubt since *McCall* v. *Poulton and another; Helphire (UK) Ltd and another intervening* [2008] EWCA Civ 1313, which was discussed at **2.4** above.

Clause 5(2) states in similar terms to the 1999 Uninsured Drivers' Agreement that the burden of proving 'knowledge' lies on the MIB, but lists a number of matters that are regarded as proof of such knowledge. Clause 5(1)(c), (2) and (4) are similar to those found in clause 6 of the Uninsured Drivers' Agreement. Once again, those sub-clauses would be subject to the interpretation of the House of Lords in *White* v. *White and the Motor Insurers' Bureau* [2001] UKHL 9 (see **Chapter 6**) and the European Court of Justice in the case of *Candolin* v. *Vahinkovakuutusosakeyhtio Pohjola* (Case C-537/03) [2006] RTR 1 (see **Chapter 5**).

Clause 5(3) (as stated above) has been omitted by the 2011 Supplementary Agreement, so as to bring the 2003 Agreement in line with the Fifth Motor Insurance Directive.

Clause 5(4) gives a number of definitions of the words used in the Agreement.

Clause 6 excludes compensation where there is insurance in place already to cover that compensation. As with the 1999 Uninsured Drivers' Agreement, the Bureau is concerned to limit its liability to those losses that are uninsured.

Clauses 7–11 set out the formal procedure for making a claim. It is very important that practitioners follow these clauses carefully because the MIB does not always follow its own procedure. By way of example, it has been known for the MIB to make an 'offer' of compensation pursuant to clause 16, which appears to be informal but is in fact a formal offer pursuant to that clause. Such a formal offer then triggers the time limit for making an appeal contained in clause 19. The MIB can make use of the 'accelerated procedure' contained in clauses 26 and 27 (see below). However, this procedure does stipulate certain time limits and, once again, the MIB does not invariably make it clear whether it is working under the formal procedure in clauses 7–11 or the accelerated procedure contained in clauses 26 and 27.

Clause 7 states that the MIB can reject a claim after a preliminary investigation. In all other cases, it conducts a full investigation. The MIB then reaches a decision which may be a refusal of the application or an award. The MIB can make an 'interim report'. This would be relevant in large value cases where it will normally take time to calculate damage. As a practical issue, it is wiser for the practitioner to get to work as soon as possible preparing the claim (on both liability and quantum) for submission to the MIB, particularly where damages are substantial. The reason is that the MIB does not behave in the same way as an insurance company. It does employ specialist staff to deal with high value claims, but if a claim is thoroughly prepared and well presented, it may be inclined to make a reasonable offer earlier rather than expending a great deal of time and expense fighting the claim. The other reason for early presentation of the claim is that once the appeal provisions in clauses 18–24 engage, the applicant runs the risk of having any award made by the MIB set aside by an arbitrator or finding him/herself under strict time limits.

Clause 8 describes how compensation is calculated. It is done in exactly the same way as a civil court would calculate damages. However, the MIB is not obliged to reimburse the applicant wages he or she has already received from his or her employer while off sick.

Clause 8(3) has been amended in line with clause 5(1) and (3) (see above). The excess of £300 still applies and there is then a specified property damage cap of £1 million.

Clause 8(4) states that the MIB does not have to pay compensation to local authorities as a result of its failure to recover a charge for the recovery, storage or disposal of an abandoned vehicle.

Clause 9 provides that interest will be awarded in the same way as a court awards interest. However, the time from which such interest will be awarded runs from the date one month after receipt by the MIB of the police report, or the date on which it would have been received if the MIB had acted promptly to obtain that report.

Clause 10 states that a 'contribution' will be made towards legal costs which are to be determined by the Schedule to the Agreement. This can be found at the end of the Agreement after clause 33. Very briefly, legal costs are calculated by reference to the amount of the award. To these are added VAT and reasonable disbursements. Paragraph 2(c) of the Schedule allows other items to be paid, but it is confusing. As we saw in **Chapter 1**, there was a typographical error in para.2(c) of the Schedule to the original 2003 Untraced Drivers' Agreement, as it appears on the MIB website. Paragraph 2(c) read 'where the applicant has opted for an oral hearing under clause and …'. This typographical error appears to have been corrected on the Directgov website version to read 'where the applicant has opted for an oral hearing under clause 28, and …'. Clause 28 deals with the referral of disputes to the arbitrator and it gives the arbitrator the power to order that one of the parties pay his fees and the costs of the proceedings. Therefore para.2(c) appears to mean that those costs may be added to the MIB's bill. However, clause 24(4) of the 2003 Untraced Drivers' Agreement also allows a fee of £500 per half day to be paid to the applicant in relation to representation if he or she betters an offer already made by the MIB, and subject to the arbitrator's order. It is submitted that para.2(c) of the Schedule includes the cost of that representation in clause 24(4) if it is awarded.

Essentially, the lack of parity between costs awarded under the 1999 Uninsured Drivers' Agreement and the 2003 Untraced Drivers' Agreement has long caused dissatisfaction among applicants and their representatives. As we will see in **Chapter 6**, a challenge was made to the absence of any proper costs award in *Evans* v. *The Secretary of State for the Environment, Transport and the Regions and the Motor Insurers' Bureau* (Case C-63/01) in the European Court of Justice. While the court criticised some aspects of what was then the 1972 Untraced Drivers' Agreement, it did not agree that the absence of costs award made it practically impossible to make an application to the MIB. More recently, in *Carswell* v. *Secretary of State for Transport and the Motor Insurers' Bureau* [2010] EWHC 3230 (APIL *PI Focus*, vol. 21, issue 3), the claimant was the widow of a man run down by an untraced driver. She accepted a settlement of £250,000 from the MIB under the 2003 Untraced Drivers' Agreement, and then sued the government asserting that:

(a)   the 2003 Agreement was systematically biased against her, in so far as it provided that only the MIB should investigate liability and quantum;
(b)   legal costs provided under the 2003 Agreement were inadequate;
(c)   the system was not equivalent to that enjoyed under civil litigation.

Hickinbottom J ruled that:

(a)   the 2003 Agreement was roughly equivalent to European Community law;
(b)   had the claimant wished to force the MIB to gather evidence and draft her schedule of loss, she could have done so;
(c)   the claimant had the option of appealing to an arbitrator on any issue;
(d)   the claimant was entitled to receive clause 10 costs, if she could prove that her lawyers had done any of the three items listed in that clause.

Clause 11 requires the applicant to use the MIB's forms and provide such information as the MIB requires. This might include an interview with the MIB under clause 11(1)(b). It also contains requirements in relation to bringing proceedings against other persons, subject to an indemnity being given by the MIB for any legal costs incurred.

Clauses 12–15 deal with the situation where there is joint and several liability, i.e. there is an untraced driver as well as a traced driver. In these clauses, the MIB set up a mechanism whereby it can recover its outlay in respect of an untraced driver against a traced driver. Practitioners should note that in such a situation, the MIB can impose a number of requirements on the claimant to co-operate with it where proceedings against the traced driver are underway. However (as with the 1999 Uninsured Drivers' Agreement), clause 11(5) of the 2003 Agreement requires the MIB to indemnify the applicant if he or she is required to bring a claim against another identified party.

Clauses 16–17 describe how the MIB communicates its decision under clause 7 to the applicant. This includes the rejection of the application, the making of an interim award and the acceptance of any decision. These clauses also include the making of structured settlement and provisional damages awards. Practitioners should note that any decision or determination made under clause 7 must be in writing and contain specified information, for instance, a statement of the MIB's reasons for its decision.

Clauses 18–24 set out the procedure for appeal and the appointment of an arbitrator. There are strict time limits for the submission of a notice of appeal. Clause 19(1) and (2) sets out the precise matters that have to be included in any such notice. Clause 20 sets out the procedure following the notice of appeal and clause 21 the procedure for the appointment of an arbitrator. Clause 22 then sets out the arbitration procedure. The applicant has the right under clause 22(4)(c) to request an oral hearing, as does the MIB. Clause 23 deals with the arbitrator's decision. Practitioners should note that a clause 23(1)(f) was added by the 2008 Supplementary Agreement to allow the arbitrator to deliberate on the issue of limitation.

The arbitrator's decision is the last stage of the MIB process. However, there is the possibility of bringing a claim under the Arbitration Act 1996. Sections 66–71 of that Act give the court certain powers in relation to an arbitration award. In particular, s.68 of the Act permits a challenge to an arbitrator's decision on the grounds of serious irregularity and s.69 on a question of law. However, these powers are highly restricted, as was shown in *Harvey* v. *Motor Insurers' Bureau* (unreported, QBD, 21 December 2011). In that case the applicant applied for leave to appeal a decision of an arbitrator under the 2003 Untraced Drivers' Agreement on liability, but Judge Hegarty QC sitting in the Mercantile Court (Manchester District Registry) refused the application, concluding that there was no point of law involved and the arbitrator was 'not obviously wrong'.

Clause 24 provides for the payment of the arbitrator's fee and the applicant's costs of legal representation. The 2003 Agreement does not say how much the arbitrator's fee is, but says that this will be agreed between the MIB and the government. Where there is an oral hearing, the MIB makes a contribution of £500 per half-day towards the cost incurred by the applicant in respect of representation by a solicitor, barrister or advocate. It is not clear whether that £500 includes VAT although the writers submit that the wording of clause 10 and the Schedule at the end of Agreement means that VAT is paid over and above the £500. From the applicant's point of view, it is important to realise that the arbitrator has the power to order the applicant (or his or her solicitor) to pay all or part of his fee if he considers that there were no reasonable grounds for bringing the appeal.

Clause 25 provides for applicants under a disability and the payment of their damages into a trust or to the Court of Protection. Practitioners should note the effect of para.3 of the Schedule to the 2003 Agreement, which requires the MIB to pay counsel's fees where the applicant is a minor or under a legal disability. See also para.3.6 of the Notes for Guidance to the 2003 Agreement.

Clauses 26 and 27 provide for an 'accelerated procedure'. This is a speedier method of disposing of a claim than the full investigation under clause 7. The majority of claims are settled by this method. There is a six-week time limit for acceptance of an offer. Use of the accelerated procedure does not prejudice a claim if an offer is refused. It is simply a speedy method of resolving claims.

Clause 28 provides a procedure for the applicant to ask for the case to be referred to an arbitrator where there is any dispute between him and the MIB concerning a decision, determination or requirement made under the Agreement, other than a dispute already covered by the procedure in clause 18. There is a four-week time limit for giving notice for the matter to be referred to arbitration.

Clause 29 provides that notices shall only be 'sufficiently served' if they are sent by fax or by registered or recorded delivery post. This rule applies to any notices or documents to be sent to the MIB. Registered post is now special delivery. However, for safety's sake, practitioners are advised to use recorded delivery. This is a somewhat cumbersome method of having to correspond with the MIB. Clearly a notice of appeal would require proof of service, but normal correspondence is another matter. Practitioners are advised to ask the MIB to waive this requirement in relation to normal correspondence.

Under clause 30, the MIB may perform any of its obligations by means of agents. In past times, it was the practice of the MIB to appoint insurance companies to deal with claims. Nowadays it tends to deal with all untraced drivers claims in-house.

Clause 31 excludes certain provisions of the Contracts (Rights of Third Parties) Act 1999, which are designed to allow a party prejudiced by the operation of a contract between two other parties to secure certain rights in relation to that contract. The 2003 Untraced Drivers' Agreement is a contract made between the government and the MIB and this clause excludes any possibility of an applicant employing the 1999 Act to sue either party. However, as we will see in **Chapter 6**, applicants have in fact sued both parties to the various Untraced Drivers' Agreements, by reliance on European Motor Insurance Directives.

Clause 32 enables the applicant to enforce payment of an award through the courts. Previously the applicant had no recourse against the MIB in an untraced driver's case. This clause is intended to be used when the MIB simply fails to deal with a claim, or it fails to pay compensation having made an award.

The Schedule to the 2003 Agreement sets out the limited costs to be paid to an applicant. Under earlier Agreements, provision for legal costs was never generous. The 1996 Untraced Drivers' Agreement only allowed for £150 plus VAT to be paid. Provided the Bureau is satisfied that the claimant obtained legal advice, it has the power to pay a contribution towards the costs of obtaining legal advice. Paragraph 2 of the Schedule says that the sum will be a percentage fee set out in the table to the Schedule, together with VAT on that fee, the £500 paid under clause 24(4) and 'reasonable disbursements'. The percentage fee is 15 per cent of the amount of the award, if that award does not exceed £150,000, subject to a minimum of £500 and a maximum of £3,000. If the award exceeds £150,000, then the percentage fee is 2 per cent of amount awarded. Therefore, an award of £200,000 would attract a percentage fee of £4,000 plus VAT together with reasonable disbursements, if there was no oral hearing. In relation to 'reasonable disbursements', the MIB has long been prepared to finance the cost of experts if it considers that the expert will provide a reasoned opinion. Paragraph 3 of the Schedule states that a disbursement can be agreed between the applicant and the MIB before it is incurred and that agreement cannot be unreasonably withheld by the MIB. Consequently there may be some merit in approaching the MIB at the time of the application and seeking to persuade it that a particular expert is suitable for the case. Such an approach may result in an unfavourable report, but it may defray a cost that the MIB might otherwise refuse to meet and so would come out of the applicant's damages.

At the end of the 2003 Agreement there are Notes for the Guidance of Victims of Road Traffic Accidents. The writers submit that these notes carry the same force as those attached to the 1999 Uninsured Drivers' Agreement. In other words, they do not supersede the terms of the 2003 Agreement, and in any event they have now been superseded by the 2008 and 2011 Supplementary Agreements.

3.4 'CLAWBACK' PROVISIONS

As with the 1999 Uninsured Drivers' Agreement, the Social Security (Recovery of Benefits) Act 1997 and the regulations made thereunder apply equally to the MIB as they do to any other defendant.

3.5 CHECK LIST FOR UNTRACED MOTORIST CLAIMS

The following check list may assist practitioners when investigating whether a claim is likely to succeed:

1. Consider evidence to show that the injury was caused by a motor vehicle.
2. Consider evidence that the motor vehicle was on a road or other public place.
3. Is the claimant vulnerable to an allegation of contributory negligence?

4. Has the claimant reported the incident to the police within the time limits set out in clause 4 of the 2003 Agreement and has the claimant co-operated fully with the police?

5. Can the application be made within the time limits set out in clause 4 of the 2003 Agreement? If not, can reliance be placed on the 2008 and 2011 Supplementary Agreements and the Memorandum of Understanding published by the MIB in relation to *Byrne*?

6. Is the application excluded under any of the exclusion provisions in the 2003 Agreement?

7. Has there been a genuine inability to trace the driver, that is, have all reasonable efforts to trace the driver been made and have they been made in a timely fashion?

8. Were there any other parties involved? If these other parties were insured, consider whether their drivers should be sued as well and ask the Bureau for an indemnity. (See clause 11(5) of the 2003 Agreement.)

9. Does the evidence suggest a deliberate or concerted act by the driver to run down the victim? In such a case, the possibility of a parallel claim under the Criminal Injuries Compensation Scheme should be considered, but see **Chapter 6** for a discussion of this issue.

CHAPTER 4

International insurance arrangements

4.1 THE GREEN CARD SYSTEM

The development of provision for victims of road traffic accidents has long been an international issue. One of the problems is ensuring the provision of compensation for a victim injured by a motorist visiting from another country. When such a visitor returns to his or her own country, the success or failure of the victim's claim could depend on whether or not there were appropriate reciprocal arrangements between the two countries.

The problem was examined in 1947 by the Economic Commission for Europe of the United Nations. The question put to various governments was whether national legislation could contemplate an agreement whereby insurers or an organisation such as the Motor Insurers' Bureau in one country would undertake to reimburse an insurance company or the bureau in another country for compensation paid to victims of road accidents.

A number of recommendations were made and as a result a 'Green Card' agreement to regulate international motor insurance was adopted by insurers in various States in November 1951.

The purpose of the Green Card system is to facilitate the cross-border movement of motor vehicles by enabling the insurance on those vehicles to meet the criteria imposed by the visited country and, in the case of accidents, to guarantee that injured parties will be compensated in accordance with the national law and regulations of that country. The international motor insurance card (Green Card) is officially recognised by the States within the system and it is proof that the vehicle so insured meets the compulsory criteria for civil liability insurance.

In each participating State a national bureau has been created and officially approved in order to provide a guarantee to:

(a) its own government that the foreign insurer will abide by the law applicable in that country and compensate injured parties within its limits;
(b) the bureau of the visited country that the member insurer will cover a claim in respect of the use of the vehicle involved in the accident.

To qualify for membership of the Green Card system, a country must first be within the geographical scope of the system, which is currently defined as 'Europe, including Russia as far east as the Urals, countries to the west of the Caspian Sea, and countries bordering the Mediterranean'. The system includes Morocco, Tunisia and Israel, as well as Iran.

The present Green Card system now applies to 45 countries in Europe and beyond. The Council of Bureaux, which is made up of national bureaux including the Motor Insurers' Bureau for the United Kingdom, is responsible for the administration and operation of the international motor civil liability system. Its website can be found at **www.cobx.org** and includes a list of current members.

The system has been governed by a series of agreements over the years. Before 29 May 2008, the bureaux were bilaterally bound by a uniform model agreement called the 'Inter-Bureaux Uniform Agreement'. In addition, some bureaux, in particular those in the European Economic Area (EEA) and other associated bureaux, were signatories of an agreement known as the 'Multilateral Guarantee Agreement'. On 29 May 2008, these agreements governing the relations between bureaux were incorporated into a single document known as the Internal Regulations.

A Green Card is not required by law to cross borders within the European Community (EC). This is because the effect of the European Motor Insurance Directives (now consolidated into the Sixth Motor Insurance Directive (2009/103/EC)) is that every EC country must ensure that any insurance policy issued in its Member State shall provide the minimum insurance cover required by law in any other EC country.

Section II of the Internal Regulations lists the countries where Green Cards are necessary for motor travel. Section III lists those non-EC countries where a Green Card is not required. On its website, the MIB advises motorists to check with their insurer to make certain that the full UK policy cover is in force when they travel abroad, whether or not a Green Card is issued. In addition, a UK insurance policy may not provide the same cover in a foreign EC country as it would in the UK, i.e. comprehensive insurance. For this reason, any motorist travelling abroad would be well advised to obtain an extension to the policy from his or her own insurer.

One of the reasons for setting up a Green Card system was to enable motorists not to be impeded in their journey by the need to comply with the differing insurance requirements of each country visited. The convenience of the motorist was taken into account by a decision not to inspect Green Cards at the internal frontiers of the countries of the EC. Some States have abolished Green Card inspection at their frontiers by virtue of agreements signed between their respective bureaux, mainly based on vehicle registration.

4.2 MOTOR INSURANCE UNDER EUROPEAN COMMUNITY LAW

The Green Card international agreement is to be distinguished from the Motor Insurance Directives that apply only to the EC and the EEA, and which were described in **Chapter 1**.

The First Motor Insurance Directive (72/166/EEC) provided for minimum levels of insurance throughout the EC. This protection has been extended by the Second, Third and Fourth Directives.

The Second Motor Insurance Directive (84/5/EC) extended compulsory cover to include both damage to property and personal injuries.

The Third Motor Insurance Directive (90/232/EEC, amending Directive 73/239/EEC) provided that compensation should be extended to untraced drivers. It also provided that the cover granted in any Member State should never be less than that granted in the home Member State.

The Fourth Motor Insurance Directive (2000/26/EC) provided further rights for victims. In line with the EC deadline, the Directive has been implemented in the UK by various statutory instruments from January 2003. One of those is the Motor Vehicles (Compulsory Insurance) (Information Centre and Compensation Body) Regulations 2003, SI 2003/37, which resulted in the setting up of the Motor Insurers' Information Centre (MIIC).

Enquiries can be made of the MIIC to locate the UK claims representatives of EEA foreign insurers if a UK resident has an accident abroad and to advise other information centres of UK insurers and their foreign claims representatives for UK accidents. The MIIC is not able to provide insurance details to enquirers over the telephone but can assist UK enquirers by post, on receipt of a signed form and a payment of £10 (including VAT) to cover the administration charge.

The 2003 Regulations have been held to confer specific rights on claimants suing foreign motorists. In *Jacobs* v. *Motor Insurers' Bureau* [2010] EWCA Civ 1208, the Court of Appeal held that the MIB should compensate a claimant injured in Spain by a German national in accordance with the law of England.

Another statutory instrument introduced following the Fourth Motor Insurance Directive is the Financial Services and Markets Act 2000 (Variations of Threshold Conditions) Order 2002, SI 2002/2707. Under this Order, motor insurers must appoint claims representatives in every EEA State. Again this creates important rights for a claimant injured by a foreign motorist in another Member State.

Regulation 11 of the 2003 Regulations states that a party resident in the UK who suffers loss or injury in a road traffic accident in an EEA State or subscribing State (other than the UK) caused by use of a vehicle which is normally based in an EEA State (other than the UK) and insured by an insurer in an EEA State (other than the UK), can bring a compensation claim against the compensation body in the UK, i.e. the MIB. The injured person can only bring a claim against the MIB if he or she has not already sued the insurer of the vehicle. There are two further conditions, either of which will allow the injured person to go straight to the MIB. Either he or she must have made a claim to the liable insurer or its representative and neither has provided a reasoned reply to the claim within a period of three months after it was made, or the insurer in question has failed to appoint a claims representative in the UK. The MIB (the compensation body for the UK) can then take steps under reg.12.

The MIB can contact the claims representative of the foreign insurer or the foreign compensation body or the person who caused the accident. It then notifies these persons/bodies that it will respond to the injured person's claim within two months. The injured person must then satisfy the MIB that he or she:

(a)   can establish liability against the other motorist; and
(b)   is entitled to damages to be assessed according to the law of that part of the UK in which he or she resides.

The European Communities (Rights Against Insurers) Regulations 2002, SI 2002/3061 were also enacted following the Fourth Motor Insurance Directive. They introduce a direct right of action against a liable insurer. However, the 2002 Regulations do not allow a claim to be brought against the insurer of a vehicle that is not normally based in the UK.

The Fifth Motor Insurance Directive (2005/14/EC) set out a number of provisions, which included an increase in the minimum compulsory insurance limit to €1,000,000 for personal injury or €5,000,000 whatever the number of victims. In the case of property damage, the minimum cover is now €1,000,000. The Directive also improved the insurance cover for persons who stayed temporarily in another Member State and it extended the role of the information centres so that they were not confined to the type of accidents referred to the Fourth Motor Insurance Directive. The case of *Schadeverzekeringen NV* v. *Jack Odenbreit* (Case C-436/06) confirms that the Fifth Motor Insurance Directive permits victims of road traffic accidents in another Member State to bring direct actions against European domiciled insurers.

The above five Motor Insurance Directives have now been consolidated into the Sixth Motor Insurance Directive (2009/103/EC).

CHAPTER 5

Rights against insurers

5.1 INTRODUCTION

The compensation system for victims of road traffic accidents in England and Wales works by way of a series of 'safety nets', which can be found in RTA 1988, the provisions of art.75 of the Articles of Association of the Motor Insurers' Bureau and the MIB Agreements themselves. As we will see in **Chapter 6**, the Criminal Injuries Compensation Scheme may also be engaged.

It is crucial that the practitioner understands how each safety net works, and that means understanding the defendant's insurance position and the liability of the insurer to pay the claimant whether by reason of:

(a)   the insurance policy;
(b)   the operation of RTA 1988; or
(c)   the provisions of art.75 referred to above.

Failure to appreciate the insurance position can lead to serious problems, particularly following the expiry of the limitation period.

A claimant who suffers injury or loss in a road traffic accident sues the tortfeasor, i.e. the person who caused the accident. That person (if insured) looks to his or her insurers to deal with the claim.

As we saw in **Chapter 1**, in the early days of motor accidents an insurer could point to a breach of the insurance policy by its own insured or use the fact of the insured's insolvency to avoid paying the innocent claimant. The Third Parties (Right Against Insurers) Act 1930 protects the victim from an insured defendant who becomes insolvent. It also enables the victim to claim against the defendant's insurer. RTA 1988, s.151 also imposes liability on a 'Road Traffic Act insurer' to pay the innocent claimant. Section 153 states that, where the insured defendant (whether an individual or a company) becomes bankrupt or falls into any of the insolvency situations outlined in s.153(2)(a)–(c), the insurer of that person or company is still obliged to satisfy the judgment obtained against it.

In order to proceed against the insurer under the 1930 or 1988 Acts, the victim has to obtain a judgment against the defendant. The claimant's rights against a liable insurer were enhanced under the European Communities (Rights against Insurers) Regulations 2002, SI 2002/3061, under which the claimant may issue proceedings against the insurer of the vehicle directly liable to him or her to the extent that it is liable to its insured. These regulations were introduced following the Fourth Motor Insurance Directive (see **1.4** and **4.2**) and they are a useful means of bringing a claim to the immediate attention of a non-responsive insurer. However, they are limited in so far as the insurer can raise against the claimant any defence that it could have raised against its insured. Furthermore, the regulations only apply to claimants resident in the European Union and certain other Member States. They also only apply to certain types of vehicles. The Fifth Motor Insurance Directive extended those rights to victims of any motor vehicle accident, but no legislation has been put in place to implement that part of the Directive.

Clause 31 of the 2003 Untraced Drivers' Agreement makes specific reference to the Contracts (Rights of Third Parties) Act 1999. Under the Act a person who is not party to a contract may in certain circumstances sue under that contract. However, the Untraced Drivers' Agreement specifically excludes the operation of the Act.

5.2 COMPULSORY INSURANCE

The Road Traffic Act 1930 was the first statute to stipulate that motorists must carry insurance against third party claims (see **Chapter 1**). The present day version, RTA 1988, states that a person must not 'use' or 'cause or permit any other person to use' a motor vehicle on a road or public place unless there is an insurance policy in force (s.143(1) of the Act).

Section 145(3)(a) says that the motor insurance policy:

> must insure such person, persons or classes of persons as may be specified in the policy in respect of any liability which may be incurred by him or them in respect of the death of or bodily injury to any person or damage to property caused by, or arising out of, the use of the vehicle on a road or other public place in Great Britain …

Section 145 goes on to specify other conditions but the wording above is the basis for the term 'compulsory insurance'. The term is important because the Bureau is only liable for accidents that, under the present legislation, must be covered by compulsory insurance. Therefore, an insurer might not be liable if the accident in question did not take place on a 'road or other public place' (i.e. on private property to which the public had no access) or in circumstances where the accident did not arise out of the 'use of the vehicle' (see **Chapter 6**).

It is possible to sue a person who fails to insure his or her own vehicle for breach of statutory duty (*Monk* v. *Warbey and others* [1935] 1 KB 75; *Norman* v. *Aziz* [2000] 52 Lloyd's Rep IR 52; *Bretton* v. *Hancock* [2005] EWCA Civ 404). This is a useful tactic in circumstances where the driver of an uninsured vehicle is unidentified, but the registered owner is identified and is refusing to co-operate.

Section 144 sets out the classes of vehicles that are not required to be insured. Briefly these are vehicles owned by local authorities, the police, salvage companies, the army, the health service and the Care Quality Commission. Practitioners will note that clause 6(1)(a) and (b) of the 1999 Uninsured Drivers' Agreement states that the Bureau is not required to compensate victims injured by Crown vehicles or by the categories of vehicle included in RTA 1988, s.144. Clause 5(1)(b) of the 2003 Untraced Drivers' Agreement states that no compensation will be paid by the Bureau for vehicles owned by, or in the possession of, the Crown.

This creates a potential gap in the compensation safety net, because if a vehicle included within s.144 is stolen by a thief or a non-employee of the authority in question, the authority that owns that vehicle can disclaim liability as can the MIB. Furthermore, clause 6(5)(a) of the 1999 Agreement states that 'a vehicle which has been unlawfully removed from the possession of the Crown shall be taken to continue in that possession whilst it is kept so removed'. This appears to mean that if a Crown vehicle is stolen, it is the Crown (not the MIB) who must pay although the Crown itself might well disclaim liability.

However, s.144 also states that the exclusion of the requirement to insure only applies to the s.144 categories of vehicle when they are under the owner's control, driven with the owner's permission or broadly being used for the purposes for which they were intended. The actual wording used is different for each class of vehicle, but it is arguable that an excluded category vehicle such as a police car driven by a thief is not being driven 'by a person employed by a police authority' and so it would be required to be insured at the time the claimant suffered his or her injury. Consequently, the MIB would be required to compensate the victim injured by such a vehicle. However, in relation to Crown vehicles, the MIB would doubtless rely on clause 6(5)(a) to avoid paying compensation.

Article 4 of the First Motor Insurance Directive allowed Member States to exempt certain vehicles from the obligation to insure, but required that compensation should be available where those vehicles caused injury outside the UK. Article 1 of the Fifth Directive (now consolidated into art.5 of the Sixth Directive) extended that requirement to injuries caused by exempt vehicles within the UK. Consequently, it is submitted that this gap breaches the terms of the Fifth Motor Insurance Directive, and an aggrieved claimant could either seek to persuade a court to interpret the MIB Agreements in line with the Directive or bring a *Francovich* action (see further **6.8** below) against the UK government (see **Chapter 1**).

Section 145(4) sets out further circumstances where no insurance is required. These are liability for the death or injury of a person in the employment of the insured, insurance for property damage exceeding £1,000,000, damage to the insured's vehicle (normally covered by a comprehensive insurance policy), damage to goods carried for hire or reward, damage to goods in the insured's custody and any 'contractual liability'. Again, these exclusions appear in the MIB Agreements, but the exclusion for liability in relation to an employee creates another potential gap if there is in fact no employment insurance at all. Section 145(4A) tries to plug this gap by saying that motor insurance will be required where there is in fact no employment insurance in place. However, the wording of s.145(4A) only protects an employee who is injured while being 'carried in or upon a vehicle' or who is 'entering or getting onto, or alighting from, a vehicle'. That would not cover an employee run over by a company vehicle driven by a thief or someone who is not an employee. Once again, a claimant in this position might be able to rely on the provisions of the Fifth Motor Insurance Directive.

5.3 ROAD TRAFFIC ACT INSURER

Where the insurance policy is valid, the insurer will simply indemnify its insured under its contract. However, situations arise where there is a breach of some contractual term, which would normally allow the insurer to avoid the policy. Section 151 of RTA 1988 restricts the circumstances in which an insurer can avoid paying the claimant, and an insurer who is caught under this section is known as a 'Road Traffic Act insurer'.

Section 151 provides the initial compensation 'safety net' for the innocent victim of an accident. If it fails, then the victim can make use of the other safety nets described below, namely art.75 of the MIB's Articles of Association and then the MIB's Agreements.

Section 151(5) says that even if the insurer is entitled to avoid or cancel the policy, or it has already avoided or cancelled the policy, it may still have to compensate the persons entitled to the benefit of a judgment. There are a number of subsections in s.151 which set out the conditions that must be fulfilled before the section can be used to compel an insurer to compensate.

Section 151(1) states that the section will apply where a certificate of insurance (or security) has been delivered under s.147 to the insured and against whom a judgment is obtained. Section 151(2)(a) states the section will apply where there is a liability covered by the insurance policy and the judgment in respect of that liability is obtained against any person who is insured by the policy. The phrase in s.151(2)(a) 'covered by the terms of the policy' means that the use to which the car was being put must be within the list of uses permitted under the actual motor insurance policy. If it is not a permitted use, then the insurer can avoid the effects of s.151.

This can cause problems for a claimant where a car insured for 'social or domestic' purposes is being hired out as a minicab. An illustration of this issue can be found in *Keeley* v. *Pashen and another* [2004] EWCA Civ 1491 (also discussed in **Chapter 6**). The claimant was a widow who brought a claim arising out of her husband's death. The defendant was a minicab driver who had driven his car deliberately at the husband. His insurance policy was limited to use only for social, domestic and pleasure purposes, but not for hire or reward. The insurer claimed that it was not liable to pay under the policy because this situation was not caught by RTA 1988, s.151. The Court of Appeal said that the defendant was not driving his car for hire or reward at the critical time, because his last fare-paying passengers of the day had left the car. After he dropped the passengers off, the essential character of his journey was to drive his car home; this was undoubtedly a purpose covered by the policy and therefore s.151 of the 1988 Act applied. The Court of Appeal also commented that social, domestic and pleasure purposes would not cover using a vehicle for a criminal purpose. The judgment does not explain why the insurer took the point as to whether it was a Road Traffic Act insurer when it should have been caught by the provisions of art.75 (see below) or at the very least the MIB should have paid the claim. However, it appears that following issue of proceedings, no notice had been given to the MIB in accordance with the 1988 Uninsured Drivers' Agreement. Consequently, the lack of proper notice appears to have been the main reason for the insurer to refuse the claim.

The scope of s.151 was also considered in *AXN and others* v. *Worboys and another* [2012] EWHC 1730 (QB) (see **Chapter 6**). The first defendant had posed as a taxi driver and he invited women into his taxi before sedating them and committing sexual assaults. He was in fact insured for both driving a taxi and for social and domestic purposes. His victims sued him for assault by poisoning, sexual assault and false imprisonment. However, they also sued the first defendant's insurers, the second defendant, pursuant to their liability under RTA 1988, s.151. One of the questions in the case was whether the first defendant's use of the vehicle at the material time was a use insured by his motor insurance policy. Silber J said that the following principles would be applicable:

- If the use was outside the permitted uses specified in the policy, it was not a liability covered by the terms of the policy for the purposes of RTA 1988, s.151.
- To determine if a use was permitted under the policy, the court had to ask itself 'what was the essential character of the journey in the course of which the particular incident occurred?' (*Seddon* v. *Binions* [1978] 1 Lloyd's Rep 381).
- The purpose had to be determined at the time when the incident occurred and not at the start of the journey.
- The critical factor must primarily be the driver's intention.
- If the essential character of the journey in question consisted of use for a criminal purpose, then the car was not being used for 'social, domestic or pleasure purposes'.

In this case, by the time the first defendant's victims were being sedated and assaulted, the primary and essential purpose of the journey was to commit sexual assaults. Consequently, it was not a use covered by the policy. The difference between this case and *Keeley* v. *Pashen* appears to be that the minicab driver in *Keeley* had stopped work for the night and was driving his car home. His decision to drive at Mr Keeley was incidental to that primary purpose. Mr Worboys' primary purpose was to assault women, not to drive his taxi.

As we will see below, an Article 75 Insurer and the MIB cannot use the distinction between social and domestic use, as opposed to business use, of the vehicle to avoid paying the innocent claimant. The MIB are required under clause 5(1) of the 1999 Agreement to pay any 'unsatisfied judgment' which means a judgment in respect of a 'relevant liability' (clause 1). That relevant liability is defined in clause 1 of the Agreement as 'a liability in respect of which a contract of insurance must be in force to comply with Part VI of the 1988 Act'. So the issue is whether there was a risk that should have been insured, not whether the risk is covered by a particular policy. Sub-paragraph (2)(a) of art.75 says that an Article 75 Insurer is still required to compensate the innocent claimant regardless of the fact that the use to which the vehicle is put is not permitted by the policy.

However, that would not have helped the claimants in the case of *AXN* because (as we will see in **Chapter 6**) the criminal sedation and assault of passengers in a taxi was not something that was required to be covered by Part VI of RTA 1988. It was not a 'use' of the vehicle.

Section 151(2)(b) of RTA 1988 then says that the section will apply where there is a liability (other than an excluded liability) 'which would be so covered if the policy insured all persons … and the judgment is obtained against any person other than one who is insured by the policy …' The effect of s.151(2)(b) is that a thief who steals an insured car will be 'covered' as against the innocent claimant by that vehicle's insurance company.

Section 151(3) states that even if the policy excludes a driver without any, or any valid, licence to drive, the insurer is still liable.

Section 151(4) defines the 'excluded liability' in s.151(2)(b) as one where the person making the claim 'was allowing himself to be carried in or upon the vehicle and knew or had reason to believe that the vehicle had been stolen or unlawfully taken …'. Section 151(4) has similarities with clause 6(1)(e) of the 1999 Uninsured Drivers' Agreement (see **Chapter 2**) and clause 5 of the 2003 Untraced Drivers' Agreement (see **Chapter 6**). In *Stych* v. *Dibble and another* [2012] EWHC 1606 (QB) it was held that the court was under an obligation to interpret RTA 1988 in a way that gave effect to the Second Motor Insurance Directive. That meant using the same restrictive interpretation of 'knowledge' used in *White* v. *White and the Motor Insurers' Bureau* [2001] UKHL 9 (see **Chapter 6**).

It is important to realise that while the road traffic legislation protects the innocent victim of an accident, it does not follow that the insurer is deprived of its contractual rights against its insured, or against the insured who lets someone else drive without valid insurance. In fact, s.151(7) and (8) specifically permit the insurer to proceed against its own insured, a person who has stolen the vehicle, and a person who causes or permits the vehicle to be used in breach of the policy. There are a number of cases where insurers have proceeded against their own insured in such circumstances, just as the MIB can acquire the right to proceed against an uninsured driver pursuant to clause 15 of the 1999 Uninsured Drivers' Agreement. See *Lloyd-Wolper* v. *Moore and another* [2004] EWCA Civ 766.

Section 151(8) excludes from the benefit of insurance a passenger who was the insured, but who has given permission to an uninsured driver to drive the vehicle. In *Churchill Insurance Co Ltd* v. *Wilkinson* [2010] EWCA Civ 556 two passengers in two separate cases were travelling in vehicles which they were insured to drive, but the negligent driver of the vehicles was uninsured but was driving with their permission. In one case permission was granted with knowledge that the driver was uninsured, and in the other the permission was granted without any thought being given to that question. The issue was whether the passengers were obliged to repay any compensation they received from the insurer of the negligent driver. The Court of Appeal considered the operation of s.151(8) as against art.13(1) of the Sixth Motor Insurance Directive. The claimants (relying on *Candolin*, below) argued that art.13(1) was intended to prevent insurers excluding from insurance cover vehicles being driven by persons unauthorised by the *insurers* and, therefore, s.151(8) was in conflict with the Directive.

A reference was made to the Court of Justice of the European Union (CJEU), formerly the ECJ. Judgment was delivered by the CJEU on 1 December 2011 in *Churchill Insurance Co. Ltd* v. *Wilkinson*; *Evans* v. *Equity Claims Ltd* (Case C-442/10). The court's principal answer was that the Directives had to be interpreted as precluding national rules, the effect of which was to 'omit automatically' the requirement that the insurer should compensate a passenger who was the victim of a road traffic accident. That was so even when that accident was caused by a driver not insured under the policy and when the victim, who was a passenger in the vehicle at the time of the accident, was insured to drive the vehicle himself and had given permission to the uninsured driver to drive it. The matter was then remitted back to the UK courts, and in *Churchill Insurance Co. Ltd* v. *Fitzgerald and Wilkinson and others* [2012] EWCA Civ 166, the Court of Appeal gave judgment. By this time, the Secretary of State for Transport had obtained permission to intervene in the appeal. Lord Justice Aikens (with whom the other members of the court agreed) said that the questions to be decided were:

(a)   whether s.151(8) could be interpreted in a way that made that section compatible with the European Directives; and

(b)   if so, how should the section be interpreted?

All the parties were agreed that it would be possible to interpret s.151(8) within the terms of the Directives by adding wording, but the dispute was about the actual wording itself. Aikens LJ said that he would interpret s.151(8)(b) as notionally including the words added in italics:

> Where an insurer becomes liable under this section to pay an amount in respect of a liability of a person who is not insured in a policy ... he is entitled to recover the amount from ... any person who ...
>
> (b)   caused or permitted the use of the vehicle which gave rise to the liability, *save that where the person insured by the policy may be entitled to the benefit of any judgment to which this section refers, any recovery by the insurer in respect of that judgment must be proportionate and determined on the basis of the circumstances of the case.*

The Court of Appeal were not asked to make any kind of determination of the cases in question, but their judgment limits the effect of s.151(8) and makes it clear that the section does not automatically exclude the insured owner/passenger who allows an uninsured person to drive his or her car from obtaining compensation from his or her insurers.

An insurer can cancel a policy of insurance. Section 152(1)(c) allows the insurer to do so, provided there is compliance with the strict requirements in that subsection.

Section 148 contains further restrictions on the right of insurers to avoid their policies. Section 148(1) states that where there is a valid certificate of insurance delivered to the insured, any part of the policy purporting to restrict the scope of the insurance by reference to a list of specified matters is of no effect as regards the existence of compulsory insurance. Section 148(2) sets out those specified matters, which are:

(a)   the age or physical or mental condition of persons driving the vehicle,
(b)   the condition of the vehicle,
(c)   the number of persons that the vehicle carries,
(d)   the weight or physical characteristics of the goods that the vehicle carries,
(e)   the time at which or the areas within which the vehicle is used,
(f)   the horsepower or cylinder capacity or value of the vehicle,
(g)   the carrying on the vehicle of any particular apparatus, or
(h)   the carrying on the vehicle of any particular means of identification other than any means of identification required to be carried by or under the Vehicle Excise and Registration Act 1994.

Furthermore, a condition stating that no liability shall arise in the event of some specified thing being done or omitted to be done after the accident shall be of no effect (RTA 1988, s.148(5)).

It should be remembered that the rules relating to compulsory insurance in RTA 1988 flow from the European Motor Insurance Directives. The ECJ has made it clear that it will not allow Member States to insert provisions into their national legislation on road traffic law which exclude claims made by claimants other than in the situations specifically provided for in the Directives.

In *Candolin* v. *Vahinkovakuutusosakeyhtiö Pohjola* (Case C-537/03) [2006] RTR 1, passengers were injured in an accident following a drinking session with the driver, who was found guilty of drunken driving together with the owner of the car who was found guilty of permitting a drunk person to drive the car. Finnish national law permitted claims to be reduced on the grounds of contributory negligence. It also specifically provided for cases involving intoxication, and the effect of this law was that none of the passengers could bring a claim because they had all been drunk and had known that the driver was drunk. The ECJ held that Members States were not permitted to include in their national legislation any exclusions from the passenger's right to compensation arising from compulsory insurance against civil liability in respect of the use of motor vehicles other than the exclusions referred to in the Directives (see Recital 23 of the Sixth Motor Insurance Directive, which makes the same point). However, that did not preclude a finding of contributory negligence by a national court. As we will see in **Chapter 6**, this has implications for both the 1999 Uninsured and 2003 Untraced Agreements.

Similarly, in *Farrell* v. *Whitty and others* (Case C-356/05) [2007] All ER (D) 140 (Apr), the claimant was travelling in a van that was not designed and constructed for the carriage of passengers in the rear of the vehicle. The driver of the van lost control of the vehicle. It later transpired that the driver was uninsured and so Ms Farrell sought compensation from the Motor Insurers' Bureau of Ireland (MIBI). The MIBI refused to compensate Ms Farrell on the grounds that she was travelling in a part of the vehicle that was not designed and constructed with seating accommodation for passengers. It took the view that liability for personal injuries sustained by her was not a liability for which insurance was compulsory under the Irish Road Traffic Act 1961. Therefore, the MIBI Agreement did not apply. The ECJ ruled that it would be contrary to the objectives of the Community legislation to exclude from the concept of 'passenger', and thus from insurance cover, injured parties seated in a vehicle which was not designed for their carriage or equipped for that purpose. Following *Farrell*, the European Commission took action against Ireland for failing to transpose art.1(4) of the Second Motor Insurance Directive (now consolidated into the Sixth Motor Insurance Directive) into Irish law (*European Commission* v. *Ireland* (Case C-211/07) [2008] All ER (D) 301). The MIBI Agreement excluded from any right to compensation for injury, any person travelling in an uninsured vehicle which collided with another uninsured vehicle. The Irish government argued that its Agreement did comply with art.1(4), but the ECJ disagreed.

5.4   GIVING NOTICE OF PROCEEDINGS TO A ROAD TRAFFIC ACT INSURER

The claimant's solicitor must give due notice to the Road Traffic Act insurer when issuing proceedings under RTA 1988, s.152(1)(a). Failure to do so means that the insurer can avoid liability and it is a further exception to the rule that the Road Traffic Act insurer must pay the claimant. The section provides that:

> No sum is payable by an insurer under sections 151 of this Act –
>
> (a)   in respect of any judgment unless, before or within seven days after the commencement of the proceedings in which the judgment was given, the insurer had notice of the bringing of the proceedings …

A letter from the claimant's solicitor is sufficient, but it must state either a clear intention to issue proceedings or that proceedings have been issued. An inference that proceedings will be issued if liability is not admitted is not sufficient. In *Wylie* v. *Wake* [2001] RTR 20 the Court of Appeal said that a prudent solicitor would be well advised to ensure that the insurer received written notice within seven days after the issue of proceedings. Consequently, it is recommended that a letter is sent shortly before proceedings by some means that can be verified, such as special delivery. Ideally, a copy of the proceedings should also be sent to the insurer immediately after issue although the present county court system (whereby proceedings for issue are sent to processing centres rather than being processed by the local court) may make that impossible. In *Desouza* v. *Waterlow* [1999] RTR 71 the court held that such notice could be given orally or in writing, but the essential purpose of the requirement of notice was that the insurer was not informed, out of the blue, that its insured had a judgment obtained against him or her. Therefore a clear and unambiguous letter before the issue of proceedings should suffice. See also *Nawaz and Hussain* v. *Crowe Insurance Group* [2003] EWCA Civ 316.

5.5 APPLICATION FOR A DECLARATION UNDER RTA 1988, SECTION 152

Section 152(2) states:

> … no sum is payable by an insurer under section 151 of this Act if, in an action commenced before, or within three months after, the commencement of the proceedings in which the judgment was given, he has obtained a declaration –
>
> (a) that, apart from any provision contained in the policy or security, he is entitled to avoid it on the ground that it was obtained –
>
> > (i) by the non-disclosure of a material fact, or
> > (ii) representation of fact which was false in some material particular, or
>
> (b) if he has avoided the policy or security on that ground, that he was entitled so to do apart from any provision contained in it

Section 152 provides the means by which an insurer can avoid paying out on the policy, but it is generally of little use to an insurer as against the innocent claimant, who will still be able to rely on either RTA 1988 or art.75 of the MIB's Articles of Association. However, it can be used against the insured who has failed to disclose some 'material fact.' A contract of insurance is a contract of the utmost good faith. A prospective policyholder is obliged to disclose to the insurer all material information affecting the risk the insurer is taking on. See *Hazel (for Lloyd's Syndicate 260, T/A KGM Motor Policies at Lloyd's)* v. *Whitlam* [2004] EWCA Civ 1600.

A s.152 declaration is also seen in cases where one insurer seeks to make the insurer of a potential co-defendant (who is partly to blame for the accident and whose insurance is entirely valid) entirely liable for the judgment.

The procedure for applying for a s.152 declaration is set out in RTA 1988, s.152(3) and (4). Notice of the application for a declaration must be served on the claimant within seven days of the judgment.

5.6 ARTICLE 75 OF THE MOTOR INSURER'S BUREAU'S ARTICLES OF ASSOCIATION

In practice, the s.152 procedure is rarely used. This is because, although an insurer is entitled to avoid a policy under the provisions of RTA 1988, it is still required to pay the claimant by reason of art.75 of the Articles of Association of the MIB, the document that governs the relationship between the MIB and its members. These Articles are updated from time to time and the latest version can be found on the MIB's website (at the time of writing they were dated 7 June 2012).

Article 75, headed 'The Domestic Regulations', is the compensation 'safety net' that generally follows when RTA 1988, s.151 is not available to assist the innocent claimant. If art.75 is not available, in the vast majority of cases where there is no insurance at all, the innocent victim should apply to the MIB.

Article 75 sets out the circumstances under which the insurers are required to pay the claimant, regardless of the invalidity of the insurance policy. That insurer will then be known as an 'Article 75 Insurer' or a Domestic Regulations insurer. Practitioners need to realise that an insurer in this position is in exactly the same position as the Motor Insurers' Bureau in so far as it can rely on the provisions of the Uninsured Drivers' Agreement. This has a number of implications for the claimant's solicitor since he or she is then bound by the provisions of the Agreement (unless these are waived) and, in particular, the requirement to give notice of proceedings under clause 9.

Article 75(2)(a) states:

> 'Article 75 Insurer' shall, subject to sub-paragraphs (a)(1)–(a)(4) of this paragraph (2), mean the Member who for the time of the accident which gave rise to a Road Traffic Act Liability was providing any insurance (other than by reason of a driving other vehicle clause) in respect of the vehicle from the use of which the liability of the judgment debtor arose.

Article75(2)(a)(1) then states:

> (1) Without prejudice to the generality of the foregoing, a Member is the Article 75 Insurer notwithstanding that:
>
> > (i)   the insurance has been obtained by fraud, misrepresentation, non-disclosure of material facts, or mistake;
> > (ii) the cover has been back dated; or
> > (iii) the use of the vehicle is other than that permitted under the policy.

Practitioners will note that the Article 75 Insurer is caught even when 'the use of the vehicle is other than that permitted under the policy' so that insurer would be required to compensate the innocent claimant even though it had insured a driver for social or domestic purposes and that driver then used the vehicle to ferry paying passengers.

Article 75(2)(a)(2) specifies the precise circumstances when an insurer ceases to be the Article 75 Insurer. There are eight, including circumstances when a policy has expired and is not intended to be renewed. Article75(2)(f) defines the 'original judgment creditor', i.e. the claimant, as:

> ... the person in whose favour a Road Traffic Act judgment was given and who is entitled to enforce it and has complied or is able and willing to comply with the conditions precedent to the Bureau's liability as set out in any of the Agreements entered into from time to time by the Bureau for the purposes of satisfying Road Traffic Act Judgments;

Therefore the Article 75 Insurer can ask that the claimant complies with the notice/other requirements of the MIB Uninsured Drivers' Agreement. However, art.75(1)(d) says:

> This Article shall be applied and interpreted in a pragmatic rather than a strictly legal manner, with a view to furthering the objectives set out in paragraph (1)(a) of this Article.

Article 75(3)(a) states that:

> If a Road Traffic Act Judgment is obtained the Article 75 Insurer will satisfy the original judgment creditor if and to the extent that the judgment has not within seven days of the execution date been satisfied by the judgment debtor.

Sub-paragraph (b) states that the member shall not be entitled to any reimbursement from the MIB. In effect this means that the liability for the accident falls on the Article 75 Insurer rather than the MIB, although the MIB still regards the Article 75 Insurer as handling the claim on its behalf.

Article 75 also contains a detailed set of provisions as to the resolution of disputes between members and the MIB. Practitioners are advised to give notice to both the Article 75 Insurer and the MIB. Article75(4) gives the Bureau the power to settle the claim while the dispute between the Article 75 Insurer/MIB is being resolved. Paragraph (7) states that the Article 75 Insurer must notify the MIB if there is a dispute as to the interpretation of the Uninsured Drivers' Agreement.

5.7 STATUS OF THE INSURER

As can be seen, the status of the defendant's insurer makes a difference to the type of notice to that insurer on the issue of proceedings and the procedure to be followed by the claimant. In the vast majority of cases there will be no issue in relation to the validity of the defendant's insurance. However, it is the authors' experience that insurance companies acting for defendants do not always take steps to ascertain their own status immediately and may well do so either shortly before the issue of proceedings or afterwards. Furthermore, an insurer may claim in correspondence that its insured has breached the policy but refuse to specify the exact nature of the breach or provide any evidence in support of its contention.

Consequently, practitioners are strongly advised, in any case where there is any doubt regarding the defendant's policy of insurance, to ask the insurer to confirm its exact status as early as possible. If it will not do so, proceedings should be issued well within limitation so as to leave open the possibility of re-issuing and giving correct notice, if (all of a sudden) the insurer claims to be an Article 75 Insurer or claims that it is not the insurer at all. In addition, clear notice should be given that proceedings are about to be issued against the insured. Consideration should be given to suing the insurer at the same time under the European Communities (Rights against Insurers) Regulations 2002, SI 2002/3061, although, if there is a breach of the policy, those regulations will not assist the claimant. However, at the very least, the issue of proceedings forces the insurer to make its position clear and seek a declaration under s.152 if it is not to be caught by s.151.

Where there is a risk that the insurer is not caught by either RTA 1988 or art.75, a formal application should be made to the MIB.

If neither the insurer nor the MIB is prepared to confirm the position, the practitioner may be obliged to issue proceedings against the defendant, his or her insurers and the MIB in accordance with the provisions of the Uninsured Drivers' Agreement. These are costly steps to take, and they should only be necessary in the most extreme cases. However, the purpose of the present legislation and the 1999 Uninsured Drivers' Agreement is to ensure that the innocent claimant receives fair and speedy compensation. Consequently, it is submitted that the costs occasioned by a refusal to give a clear indication as to its status, or indeed its failure to determine its responsibility with the MIB should be paid by that insurer.

In cases where the insurer has confirmed art.75 status, the practitioner should ascertain, before issuing proceedings, whether he or she is required to follow the steps set out in the Uninsured Drivers' Agreement, which may include adding the insurer to the proceedings.

CHAPTER 6

Cases involving or affecting the Bureau

This chapter deals with the attitude taken by the courts on the activities of the Bureau in the interpretation of the Motor Insurers' Bureau Agreements and also on the approach taken by the Bureau with regard to claims made under the Agreements.

6.1 IS THE CLAIM COVERED BY THE MOTOR INSURERS' BUREAU AGREEMENTS?

When dealing with a new claim, the first consideration for the Bureau is whether it falls within the terms of the Agreements. As we saw in **Chapter 5**, s.145(3)(a) of the Road Traffic Act 1988 states that a motor insurance policy:

> must insure such person, persons or classes of persons as may be specified in the policy in respect of any liability which may be incurred by him or them in respect of the death of or bodily injury to any person or damage to property caused by, or arising out of, the use of the vehicle on a road or other public place in Great Britain …

This is the minimum scope of compulsory insurance for which the Bureau is liable to compensate the innocent claimant. Consequently, the Bureau will refuse to pay compensation to any victim of a motor accident where the liability was not caused by, or did not arise out of, the use of the vehicle on a road or other public place in Great Britain.

For example, as we will see below, the Bureau may decide that the particular 'use' of a vehicle is not something that should be covered by insurance because it involved a criminal act. Furthermore, a motor accident that does not take place on a road or public place is not covered by the Agreements because such an accident is not required to be covered by compulsory insurance. Likewise, the Bureau will refuse to compensate a passenger riding in an uninsured vehicle if it can prove that person 'knew' that the vehicle was uninsured because that is a situation specifically excluded by the 1999 Agreement. The same exclusion appears in the 2003 Untraced Drivers' Agreement. Practitioners should realise that insurance companies sometimes take the same points as against a claimant, so for instance a person who climbs into an insured vehicle knowing that the driver has no licence may be unable to claim compensation if the insurance company can establish that he or she 'knew' that the driver was not covered by the insurance policy.

6.2 'USE' OF THE VEHICLE

The definition of 'use' tends to arise frequently in claims on the Bureau, but the principle is the same for cases involving insurers. There are two main areas of 'use' where the Bureau will refuse to compensate. The first is where a person claiming compensation is in fact held to be using the vehicle him/herself and the second is where the vehicle is used as a weapon or to commit some crime.

In relation to the first area, 'use' can include use of the car by a passenger at the time of the accident, or a situation where the driver and the passenger are involved in a joint criminal enterprise. Practitioners should note that in the case of passengers 'using' a vehicle, the Bureau will sometimes also seek to argue that the claimant knew that there was no insurance on the vehicle, as well as putting forward the defence of contributory negligence. We deal with the issue of 'knowledge' later in this chapter. Caution needs to be exercised with these cases in light of decisions such as *Candolin* v. *Vahinkovakuutusosakeyhtiö Pohjola* (Case C-537/03) [2006] RTR 1 (see **5.3**) and *White* v. *White* [2001] UKHL 9 (see below).

The following are a sample of the numerous cases that demonstrate the sometimes surprisingly wide scope of 'use' in this context.

Stinton v. *Stinton* [1995] RTR 167 – the uninsured defendant who had bought a car set off with a passenger. Both were drunk. The issue arose as to whether the passenger was 'using the vehicle'. It was held that he was. His claim had actually been reduced by one-third on the ground that he was partly to blame. Furthermore, it was found that both driver and passenger had embarked on the 'common object' of driving an uninsured vehicle. Therefore the Bureau could avoid liability.

Hatton v. *Hall* [1997] RTR 212 – the court had to consider whether the claimant, a pillion passenger on a motorbike, was a 'user' of the vehicle. The court asked: 'Is there a sufficient degree of control or management of the vehicle to make a claimant a user of the vehicle?' On the facts of this case, it was held that there was not.

O'Mahoney v. *Joliffe and Motor Insurers' Bureau* [1999] RTR 245 – the court considered the meaning of the term 'using' and said that:

(a) the term 'using' in clause 6 of the 1988 Uninsured Drivers' Agreement had the same meaning as in RTA 1988, and therefore the term 'user' had a restricted meaning;

(b) a passenger was not necessarily a user, even if he or she knew that the vehicle was uninsured, but knowledge of no insurance might count towards the conclusion that the passenger was in fact a user of the vehicle;

(c)   an element of control, management or operation of the vehicle was required on the part of the passenger;

(d)   the procurement of the venture by the passenger or an element of joint enterprise would sometimes give rise to the necessary element of control;

(e)   the question in (d) above was one of fact and degree for the judge.

In this case the passenger had actually ridden the bike at one stage herself. She was held to be a user and, in any event, she knew that there was no insurance.

Dunthorne v. *Bentley* [1996] RTR 428, CA – the defendant's car broke down after running out of petrol. She crossed the road to fetch a friend to help out and was hit by an oncoming vehicle. The driver suffered injury and sued her. The defendant's insurers were ordered to pay damages as the accident had arisen out of her 'use' of the vehicle.

Cawthorn v. *Director of Public Prosecutions* [2000] RTR 45 – the defendant motorist parked and left his car with the hazard lights on outside a private residence while he posted a letter. During his absence, the car rolled downhill, possibly due to the mischievous release of the handbrake by a passenger, and collided with a brick wall, causing damage. The question for the Court of Appeal was whether the defendant had been 'driving' the car at the time, and it found that he was so driving. The statutory obligation imposed by RTA 1988, s.170 would still apply if the accident was caused by the presence of the vehicle on the road whether or not it was being driven by the driver at the material time, and even though there was a break in his driving.

Slater v. *Buckinghamshire County Council; Slater* v. *Stigwood (trading as Stig-woods (a firm)) and another* [2004] All ER (D) 287 (Jan) – the claimant was a Down's syndrome patient. The local authority's minibus sub-contractor would pick him up every day from his home to take him to the day centre. Normally the claimant would wait for the minibus on the opposite side of the road to his home. On the day of the accident, the driver of the minibus pulled up outside the house on the opposite side of the road at which point the escort who was also in the minibus got ready to get out and collect the claimant. However, before the claimant's escort could collect him, he came out of his house and ran suddenly across the road into the path of a car. The car driver was exonerated of any blame. The claimant's lawyers tried to argue that either the local authority or its sub-contractor were at fault. The reasoning behind their argument was that the claimant had been injured as a result of the 'use' of the minibus. Consequently, this was a situation where s.145(3) of RTA 1988 applied and the local authority and/or the sub-contractor's insurance had to cover the accident. Morland J said:

> The person who must be insured is the user of the vehicle … the user of the vehicle is a limited class of persons, the driver, his employer or his principal and the owner of the vehicle. 'User' does not include passengers including fellow employees of the driver who

may have duties to perform on the vehicle in relation to passengers in the vehicle or boarding or alighting from the vehicle.

Therefore, the driver of the minibus could be a user but the claimant's escort was not. The injury to the claimant did not arise out of the use of the minibus. The escort was a passenger who had got out of the vehicle and the claimant was a passenger who intended to get into the vehicle. Any liability on the sub-contractor would thus be a public liability not a motor liability.

Bretton v. *Hancock* [2005] EWCA Civ 404 – the 'user' of the vehicle was its owner who allowed her car to be driven by an uninsured driver (although she thought that he was insured at the time). The definition of 'use' came down to whether the claimant was in fact the owner of the car.

Turner v. *Green and another* [2008] EWHC 3133 (QB) – a motorcycle owned by the first defendant was being driven along a road and crashed into a wall. The claimant (who claimed that he was a passenger) was thrown from the motorcycle and suffered serious injuries. The central issue was whether the claimant was a pillion passenger on the motorcycle or the driver. It was found that he was the driver and his claim was dismissed. On the evidence, the claimant had been drinking on the day of the accident and it was highly likely that he was unfit to drive. He asked and was given permission to ride the motorcycle. He did so and as he approached a bend in the road he lost control, probably as a result of the influence of alcohol and his lack of any recent experience of riding a powerful motorcycle, and collided with the kerb and a brick wall.

The second area where 'use' is held to debar the claimant from compensation from the Bureau is where that use is intended to injure another person. It is settled law that even though the use of an uninsured vehicle to injure a person may be deliberate or criminal, the Bureau may still be liable to pay the injured person. If there is an insurer for the vehicle, the claim may be brought against that insurer either under art.75 of the Bureau's Articles of Association or RTA 1988 (see **Chapter 5**).

The forerunner to the 2003 Untraced Drivers' Agreement in 1996 contained a clause to the effect that deliberate acts were excluded from compensation by the Bureau. However, neither the present 1999 Uninsured Drivers' Agreement nor the 2003 Untraced Drivers' Agreement specifically exclude criminal acts from their scope. Both Agreements rest on the concept of compensation for an accident that would have come within the scope of compulsory insurance, as defined above.

The following cases demonstrate how the scope of compulsory insurance may include the use of a vehicle to commit a criminal act.

Hardy v. *Motor Insurers' Bureau* [1964] 2 QB 745 – a security officer, noticing a stolen road fund licence on a van belonging to a fitter, waited for the van at a point where the private road through his employers' property joined the main road. He tried to stop the driver by putting his head in at the window and asking the driver to pull up at the side of the road. The driver drove off at speed, dragging the claimant on his knees to the main road. The security officer fell off while the car was on the main road. The driver was charged with, and found guilty of, driving without a licence or insurance and causing grievous bodily harm. In subsequent civil proceedings against the driver, judgment was entered by consent for £300 damages.

The judgment being unsatisfied, the claimant brought proceedings against the Bureau, which defended the claim to on basis that it arose out of a wilful and deliberate criminal act and that, as such, the claim would not be covered by a policy of insurance, even had there been such a policy in existence.

The Court of Appeal held that insurance cover, being compulsory for liability arising out of the use of the vehicle by the insured on a road, would include 'murderous' or 'playful' use. Therefore, even though the driver was guilty of a felony under s.18 of the Offences Against the Person Act 1861, and, as between the insurer and the driver, liability might have been denied (i.e. the driver could not recover from his insurers), this would not have affected the claimant's claim against the driver himself. Under s.207 of the Road Traffic Act 1960 (now RTA 1988, s.151), the claimant would be able to claim against the insurers, notwithstanding the fact that the claim arose out of the wilful and culpable act of the insured.

Gardner v. *Moore* [1984] AC 548 – the House of Lords, in declining an invitation to overrule *Hardy* v. *Motor Insurers' Bureau*, held the Bureau liable to pay damages to a pedestrian deliberately run down by a driver who later pleaded guilty to a charge under s.18 of the Offences Against the Person Act 1861.

Charlton v. *Fisher and another* [2001] EWCA Civ 112 – the claimant was a passenger in a car into which the first defendant deliberately reversed his car. He later pleaded guilty to criminal damage. The incident occurred in the car park of a hotel. The first defendant's insurers refused to indemnify him. One ground for resisting the claim was that it was contrary to public policy to permit an insured to recover an indemnity in respect of his own deliberate criminal act. The Court of Appeal agreed, restating that the general principle that a person should not gain an advantage arising from the consequences of *his own* iniquity applied in relation to motor insurance contracts as it did elsewhere. However, the Court of Appeal stressed that the claimant would have had recourse against the insurer under RTA 1988, s.151 or to the Bureau if the accident had occurred on a road. Unfortunately for the claimant, the accident had occurred on 5 October 1995 before the introduction of the Motor Vehicles (Compulsory Insurance) Regulations 2000, SI 2000/726, which would have brought the car park in question within the scope of a 'public place' and so the claimant's 'accident' would have been within the scope of compulsory insurance (see **Chapter 5**).

Keeley v. *Pashen and another* [2004] EWCA Civ 1491 – the claimant was the widow of a man killed by a vehicle driven by an irate taxi driver after an altercation in his minicab. The defendant's insurance policy was issued by Wren Motor Syndicate 1202 and was limited to 'Use only for social, domestic and pleasure purposes including travel to and from permanent place of business …'. The policy did not cover using the car as a minicab. Wren said that it was not liable to pay under the policy because it was not an insurer for the purposes of RTA 1988. The Bureau was not involved as it had not been given notice of proceedings. The Court of Appeal held that the defendant was not driving his car for hire and reward at the critical time, because his last fare-paying passenger of the day had left the car. After he dropped the claimant's husband and his friends off, the essential character of his journey was to drive his car home, and this was undoubtedly a purpose covered by the policy. Brooke LJ commented that, if the essential character of the journey in question consisted of use for a criminal purpose (as when a burglar takes his car out for a night of burgling other people's houses), then the car would not be being used for 'social, domestic and pleasure purposes', but that was not the case here.

The court made a similar decision in *Bristol Alliance Ltd Partnership* v. *Williams and another* [2011] EWHC 1657 (QB) where Tugendhat J held that a claimant was entitled to recover against a defendant insurer even though the damage was the result of a deliberate act by the defendant insured as part of his attempt to commit suicide.

The possibility of claiming against an insurer for the deliberate acts of its insured is limited. In *AXN and others* v. *Worboys and another* [2012] EWHC 1730 (QB), the first defendant was convicted of a number of offences including administering a substance with intent, and committing various sexual assaults while acting as a taxi driver. His victims sued him for assault by poisoning, sexual assault and false imprisonment. However, they also sued the first defendant's insurers, the second defendant, pursuant to its liability under RTA 1988, s.151. The trial centred on the preliminary issue of whether the insurers were liable. As we saw in **5.3**, Silber J considered whether the first defendant's assaults were covered by his policy of insurance. If they were, the insurers might be liable to compensate the claimants under s.151. The answer to that question was in the negative because the assaults could not be said to be within the scope of the policy.

However, there was a further question, which was whether the assaults against the claimants were covered by the definition of 'compulsory insurance' under RTA 1988, s.145. This meant asking whether they constituted 'bodily injury to any person … caused by, or arising out of, the use of the vehicle on a road or other public place' within the meaning of RTA 1988, s.145(3)(a). If the assaults did come within s.145(3)(a), then as with *Hardy*, claimants in this kind of situation might have a claim against an Article 75 Insurer or the MIB. What actually happened in *AXN* was that the claims were brought against the insurers under s.151. There was no claim against the MIB or the insurers under art.75.

Silber J referred to *Dunthorne* v. *Bentley* [1996] RTR 428 (see above). The principles that emerged from that case were:

(a)   that the concept of 'arising out of' was a wider concept than 'caused by';
(b)   the focus of the inquiry should be to consider whether the injuries of the claimants were matters arising out of the use of the car; and
(c)   that it was necessary to analyse the activities of the driver. Reference was also made to *Slater* v. *Buckinghamshire County Council* (see above).

Silber J considered that the correct approach should be as follows:

• The term 'arising out of' contemplated more remote consequences than those envisaged by the words 'caused by' and extended the test, with the result that it included less immediate consequences.

• 'Arising out of' did not mean a proximate or an effective cause as this was too narrow a test.

• The term 'arising out of' still excluded the use of the vehicle being casually concomitant but not casually connected with the act in question.

• The relationship to which the words 'arising out of' had to be applied was between the injuries suffered (not the negligent and wrongful acts) and the use of the vehicle not at the start of the journey but at the time when the injuries were suffered.

• The application of the words 'bodily injury … arising out of the use of a vehicle' entailed considering all the material circumstances.

• The purpose of the user of the motor vehicle was relevant in deciding whether what occurred and, in particular, the bodily injuries, arose out of the use of the vehicle.

• The focus had to be on the question of whether the bodily injury of the claimant was a matter arising out of the use of the vehicle at the time when the bodily injuries were sustained.

The chain between the first defendant's use of the taxi and the claimants' injuries was broken by the first defendant's acts of poisoning and committing sexual assaults. There was no link between the injuries suffered by the claimants and the use of the taxi on a road when the claimants were poisoned and assaulted. In *Dunthorne* the injuries were caused because the defendant wished to continue her journey by car but could not do so without crossing the road to get more petrol. In *AXN*, the claimants came by their injuries not because they wished to continue their journeys, but because the first defendant wished to poison and then assault them. The cases of *Hardy*, *Gardner* and *Bristol* were examples not merely of bad driving, but of deliberately using a car as a weapon, whereas the injuries sustained by the claimants in *AXN* did not arise out of the use of Worboys' taxi on the road.

Consequently, the second defendants were not liable under RTA 1988, s.151 to compensate the claimants. As we saw in **Chapter 5**, if the claimants had sued the MIB or an Article 75 Insurer, their claims would have failed because the assaults did not come under the definition of 'compulsory insurance' in RTA 1988.

6.3 CLAIMS TO THE CRIMINAL INJURIES COMPENSATION AUTHORITY

As we saw above, neither the present 1999 Uninsured Drivers' Agreement nor the 2003 Untraced Drivers' Agreement specifically exclude criminal acts from their scope. Cases such as *Hardy* enable a claimant to make a claim against the Bureau even where the use of the vehicle was deliberately to injure him or her.

However, the victim of a deliberate or criminal act involving a motor vehicle has the right to make a claim to the CICA and a practitioner in this situation should consider making such a claim parallel to that on the MIB. There are circumstances where the CICA may provide the only source of compensation for the claimant, for instance, where there is doubt as to whether the incident has occurred on a road or other public place, or whether it arose out of the 'use' of the vehicle (see above).

Criminal injuries caused by vehicles may be covered under the terms of the Criminal Injuries Compensation Scheme 2008. Paragraph 11 of the 2008 Scheme states:

> A personal injury is not a criminal injury for the purposes of this Scheme where the injury is attributable to the use of a vehicle, except where the vehicle was used so as deliberately to inflict, or attempt to inflict, injury on any person ...

This would appear to exclude cases of negligent or reckless driving. In *R (on the application of Tait)* v. *Criminal Injuries Compensation Appeals Panel* [2009] All ER (D) 72 (Apr) the claimant was a police officer, injured when the driver of the stolen car rammed his vehicle twice. In May 2003 he applied to the CICA for compensation. His claim was rejected as the Criminal Injuries Compensation Appeals Panel (CICAP) concluded that the applicant's own view that the driver of the stolen car was trying to injure him was not supported by evidence. He sought judicial review of that Panel's decision. In the High Court, Stadlen J said that if a vehicle was used to ram another car for the purpose of causing so much damage to it as to disable it, that was not necessarily inconsistent with a finding that the car was being used as a weapon. The intention here was to hit the claimant's car with such force as to disable it. Although injuring the claimant was not the motive of the criminal, it was his intention. Therefore, in those circumstances, it did seem that it was intended that a person in the position of the claimant would fall within the class of persons who were eligible for compensation under the Criminal Injuries Compensation Scheme. It is not clear why the claim in that case could not have been made to the Bureau under the principle in cases such as *Hardy* and *Gardner*.

The Criminal Injuries Compensation Scheme applies a tariff for injuries, with an upper limit of £500,000 and pays no costs. Therefore, a claim to the Bureau will be always be the more attractive option. Practitioners should also note that both the Bureau and the CICA have the right (when awarding compensation) to take into account any compensation paid to a victim from some other source. The prudent course when dealing with any claim involving the potential criminal use of a car is to make two claims, one to the Bureau and the other to the CICA. The CICA should then be invited to await the result of the claim to the Bureau.

6.4 'ROAD OR OTHER PUBLIC PLACE'

The liability of the Bureau is restricted to the use of a vehicle on a road within the definition in RTA 1988, s.192. The Act defines a 'road' as 'any highway and any other road to which the public has access, and includes bridges over which a road passes'. On 3 April 2000, the Motor Vehicles (Compulsory Insurance) Regulations 2000, SI 2000/726, amended RTA 1988, s.143 by extending the offence of using, or causing or permitting someone to use, a motor vehicle on a road unless its use was covered by an appropriate policy of insurance or security, to the use of a vehicle on a road *or other public place*.

Consequently the cases that follow (most of which pre-date the 2000 Regulations) should be read in the light of the current law and many would almost certainly be decided differently today. Some of these cases relate to prosecutions in the magistrates' court for such offences as use of a vehicle without a current MOT certificate; parking without lights; or driving an unroadworthy vehicle – all involving a vehicle being used on a 'road'. At the same time, the pre-2000 cases are still important in post-2000 cases because, whether the accident takes place on a road or other public place, the issue is still about public access. The following are a selection of the many cases on this issue.

Harrison v. *Hill* [1932] JC 13 – the court said that the test was whether the public actually and legally enjoyed access to the road in question. That could be access permitted or allowed, expressly or implicitly, by the person to whom the road belonged. Lord Clyde said (at para.16):

> I think that when the statute speaks of 'the public', what is meant is the public generally and not the special class of members of the public who has occasion for business or social purposes to go to the farmhouse or any part of the farm itself ... There must be, as a matter of fact, walking or driving by the public on the road and such walking and driving must be lawfully performed – that is to say, must be permitted or allowed, either expressly or implicitly, by the person or persons to whom the road belongs.

Bugge v. *Taylor* [1941] 1 KB 198 determined that a forecourt used as a short cut was a road.

Thomas v. *Dando* [1951] 1 All ER 1010 – the court decided that an unpaved forecourt, adjoining the pavement but forming part of a private garden, was not a road.

Purves v. *Muir* [1948] JC 122 – the court decided that a farm road to which there was public access, a drive leading from a public road to a private house, and a forecourt providing access to a hotel, were all roads.

Buchanan v. *Motor Insurers' Bureau* [1955] 1 WLR 488 – the claimant had successfully sued a lorry driver for negligence. The accident had occurred on premises belonging to the Port of London Authority. The issue raised was whether the premises constituted a 'road' for the purposes of the Road Traffic Acts. McNair J gave judgment for the Bureau on the basis that the premises were not in a place to which the general public had access by right or by tolerance of the Port of London Authority.

Griffin v. *Squires* [1958] 1 All ER 468 – a car park providing access for allotment holders and members of a private bowling club to a private path leading to the club was not a road. The court refused to adopt the *Oxford Dictionary* definition, which is 'a line of communication between places for the use of foot passengers, riders and vehicles'. Streatfield J said:

> I have to give proper effect to the words of the Act of Parliament. Although a car park is, in my opinion, a line of communication, I do not think that anybody in the ordinary acceptance of the word 'road' would think of a car park as a road. If we were to hold that this was a road, a piece of waste land by the side of the road to which the public could resort for picnics would also have to be a road, and nobody would call that a road.

Randall v. *Motor Insurers' Bureau* [1969] 1 All ER 21 – a school caretaker had been instructed by the headmaster of the school to see that a site which was being cleared for building at the rear of the school was not used for further unauthorised tipping of rubbish. A lorry driver was about 12 yards on the site when Mr Randall told him he would be reported to the police. The lorry driver became abusive and Mr Randall walked to the side entrance. The lorry driver moved forward, straight at Mr Randall, with the engine roaring. Mr Randall jumped to his left, but was caught on his right leg by the lorry's wing and trapped between the moving lorry and the escarpment of a raised bank. This initially caused no substantial injury but, as the lorry passed him, he was pulled forward and fell to the ground. The offside rear wheel of the lorry went over his left leg, while the front wheels were out into the road. The lorry driver then drove off. Mr Randall obtained judgment in a civil action against the driver for damages assessed at £1,073 and costs, which were taxed at £243. The lorry driver's insurers repudiated liability and the Bureau, in accordance with its usual practice in such cases to save unnecessary costs of third party litigation, agreed that the action could be brought against it without the insurers being joined. Megaw J held that the injuries arose out of a vehicle on a road and that the damages awarded under the judgment against the lorry driver were therefore recoverable under the relevant Agreement.

Adams v. *Metropolitan Police Commissioner* [1980] RTR 289 – a private housing estate, Aberdeen Park in London, was used as a shortcut by pedestrians and also as a racetrack by youths on motorcycles. The police refused to prosecute on the basis that the estate was not a road within the meaning of s.196(1) of the Road Traffic Act 1972. The claimants brought an action for a declaration that the private road known as 'Aberdeen Park, London N5' was a highway or other road to which the public has access within the meaning of s.196(1) of the Act. Jupp J found that Aberdeen Park was, on the evidence, a road to which the public had access within the meaning of the Road Traffic Act 1972.

Oxford v. *Austin* [1981] RTR 416 (Divisional Court) – Kilner Brown J approached the problem of defining a road in two parts. He said:

> The first question which has to be asked is whether there is in fact, in the ordinary understanding of the word road, that is to say, whether or not there is a definable way between the two points over which vehicles could pass. The second question is whether or not the public, or a section of the public, with access to that which has the appearance of a definable way. If both questions can be answered affirmatively, there is a road for the purpose of the various Road Traffic Acts and Regulations.

Curran v. *McCormick and the Motor Insurers' Bureau* [1996] 4 BNIL, CA – the claimant had been in a public house drinking with the first defendant and another person. They all left in a car driven by the first defendant, who was not insured. There was a near collision with a police car which developed into a police chase. This came to an end when the car was driven off the road, through a farmyard, an orchard, across fields and through a steel gate before ending up in a ditch. The claimant brought a claim against the first defendant and the MIB. The court held that it could not possibly be said that the injuries had arisen from driving on the public road and consequently the Bureau was not liable. It should be noted that the Bureau also maintained the defence that the claimant 'knew' that the car was uninsured and furthermore that he was 'using' it (see below) even though he was a passenger.

Cutter v. *Eagle Star Insurance Co. Ltd; Clarke* v. *Kato and others* [1999] RTR 153, 163 JP 502 – Lord Clyde said at para.161(B) of his judgment:

> … the question is raised whether one or other or both of the car parks qualifies as a road. In the generality of the matter it seems to me that in the ordinary use of language a car park does not so qualify. In character and more especially in function they are distinct. It is of course possible to park on a road, but that does not mean that the road is a car park. Correspondingly one can drive from one point to another over a car park, but that does not mean that the route which has been taken is a road. It is here that the distinction in function between road and car park is of importance. The proper function of a road is to enable movement along it to a destination. Incidentally a vehicle on it may be stationery. One can use a road for parking. The proper function of a car park is to enable vehicles to stand and wait. A car may be driven across it; but this is only incidental to the principal function of parking.

At para.163A, he went on to say:

> The word 'road' is plainly intended to cover all kinds of road. It embraces not only highways but also 'any other' roads. So a considerable breadth of meaning is available, provided that the place still qualified as a 'road'.

Sadiku v. *Director of Public Prosecutions* (1999) *The Times*, 3 December – the court was called upon to decide whether Trafalgar Square is a road. Quite unsurprisingly the court held that it was, reiterating that a decision whether or not a particular place was a road was one of fact for the magistrates at first instance.

Planton v. *Director of Public Prosecutions* [2002] RTR 9 – the defendant was seen by the police in the driving seat of a stationary vehicle with the engine running and lights on, halfway across a causeway linking Decoy Point and Osea Island in Essex. He was breathalysed and found to be over the limit. He was convicted of driving with excess alcohol, contrary to RTA 1988, s.5(1)(a). The court at first instance held that the causeway was a public place because the public had access to it and the defendant was driving at the relevant time. The Court of Appeal held that although the use of the causeway was to provide access to the residences on the island, there was no evidence of any general public access to the island for any purpose and that accordingly the evidence was insufficient to entitle the justices to conclude that this was a public place.

Brewer v. *Director of Public Prosecutions* [2005] RTR 5 – Mr Brewer was seen by the police driving his car slowly but erratically in a railway station car park. He had excess alcohol in his blood and was a disqualified driver. He tried to argue that at the time he had not been driving on a 'road' and therefore was not caught by the offences defined under RTA 1988, ss.5(1) and 103(1). The peculiarity of this case was that the Crown Prosecution Service did not bring a specific charge against the defendant that he had been driving in a 'public place'. However, the prosecutor invited the court to hold that the car was on a 'road'. The evidence showed that the car park was bordered partly by a fence and had a gate at the entrance. Vehicular access was gained by pressing a button to produce a ticket and the removal of the ticket in turn caused the barrier to lift. Access to one of the railway staff car parks was obtained through the car park, and pedestrian access to a station platform could be gained from the car park by users of the car park and members of the general public. The justices concluded that the railway station car park constituted a road and convicted the defendant on this basis. Mr Brewer appealed successfully to the Court of Appeal who decided that the car park was not a road. Practitioners should note that a car park of this nature would almost certainly be a public place for the purposes of RTA 1988, since the introduction of the 2000 Regulations.

Evans v. *Clarke and NIG Insurance plc* [2007] Lloyds Law Reports IR 16 – in this case Mr Clarke ran a business repairing camper vans. He was insured by NIG under a motor trade risk policy. In July 2002 there was an accident when a VW camper van owned by Mr Clarke ran backwards down a ramp into the claimant, Mr Evans. Mr Clarke's workshop was located on an industrial estate in Swansea. To gain access to the workshop, vehicles had to travel up a small ramp at a right angle to the left-hand side of the road that ran past the workshop. On the day of the accident Mr Clarke was winching up a camper van. Mr Evans was driving past the workshop, wanting to go to the next-door unit, but he had to stop in front of Mr Clarke's ramp. He got out of his vehicle and it was then that the camper van ran backwards, trapping him between the two vehicles. NIG refused to indemnify Mr Clarke. One of its objections was that the accident had not occurred on a road to which the public had access. The issue related to the definition of 'road' in the policy. NIG contended that since the public did not have access to the road alongside Mr Clarke's workshop, it was not a road. Field J said that, having regard to the policy as a whole, 'road' in the coverage provision had the same meaning as that found in RTA 1988, in other words, a road to which the public had access. The use of the definite article in the policy 'on the road' connoted public rather than private access. Field J had visited the industrial estate on which Mr Clarke's workshop was situated and he described the layout in detail. There were access roads that were private and unadopted on the estate and large steel gates at the entrance that were opened early in the morning and closed in the evening. He considered a number of cases that had been cited to the court including *Harrison* v. *Hill* [1932] JC 13 and *R* v. *Spence* (unreported, CA, 23 March 1999). In this case the industrial park contained a number of units whose occupiers were sure to desire members of the public to come and do business with them without having first to make an appointment. The public did so without having to obtain access by overcoming a physical obstruction or in defiance of a prohibition, express or implicit. There was nothing to suggest that either Mr Clarke or his neighbour were only prepared to do business with a select group of people. Consequently, the accident had occurred on a road within the terms of the policy.

6.5 'MOTOR VEHICLE'

The claimant must be injured by a motor vehicle. A 'motor vehicle' is defined in RTA 1988, s.185(1) as 'a mechanically propelled vehicle intended or adapted for use on roads'. The Bureau will not pay out to the victims of accidents caused by uninsured bicycles or horses. There is often a problem where victims are hit by scrambler motorcycles or buggies. The following are a selection of the many cases that demonstrate the courts' approach to this issue.

Daley v. *Hargreaves* [1961] 1 All ER 552 – the court said that 'intended' (for use on roads) might be interpreted as 'suitable' or 'apt'. It was held that dumper trucks not fitted with windscreens, lamps, reflectors, horns, wings and number plates did not come within the definition.

Burns v. *Currell* [1963] 2 All ER 297 – a go-kart was regarded as not falling within the definition of 'motor vehicle'. The vehicle had an engine at the rear, with a tubular frame mounted on four small wheels and was equipped with a single seat, steering wheel and column and an efficient silencer. Its brakes operated on the rear wheels only. It had no horn, springs, parking brakes, driving mirror or wings. There was evidence before the court that it had been used on the road on only one occasion. There was no evidence that other go-karts were used on the road. Again, the Divisional Court applied a test equivalent to a matter-of-fact jury approach:

> There was not sufficient evidence … to prove beyond a reasonable doubt that any *reasonable person* [author's italics] looking at the go-kart would say that one of its uses would be a use on the road nor that it was fit or apt for use on the road although it was capable to full use.

Chief Constable of Avon & Somerset v. *Fleming* [1987] 1 All ER 318 – the test was whether a reasonable person would say, looking at the vehicle, that its general use encompassed possible general road use. That case involved a scrambler motorbike, which did not come within the definition of a mechanically propelled vehicle intended or adapted for use on roads.

Director of Public Prosecutions v. *Saddington* [2001] RTR 15 – the defendant, who was disqualified, passed through a red traffic light while riding an unregistered motorised scooter known as a 'Go-Ped' on a road. It was powered by a 22.5 cc engine with a maximum speed of 20 mph. The scooter had faulty steering and no lights, suspension, clutch or controls to enable the rider to control the machine. The Court of Appeal held that the test of whether the Go-Ped was a 'motor vehicle' as defined by RTA 1988, s.185(1) was whether a reasonable person looking at the vehicle would say that one of its uses would be use on the roads. In deciding that question, the reasonable person had to consider whether some general use on the roads might be contemplated. The roadworthiness of a vehicle, namely its capability to be used safely on a road, was not decisive on the question of whether its use on the roads was contemplated. The test was not whether a reasonable person would use the vehicle on a road. It had to be intended for a road, since it would not travel over uneven surfaces. There was a considerable temptation to use the vehicle on a road, given the fact that it could get through traffic. This was despite the fact that the distributor's literature said quite clearly that the vehicle was not intended for road use.

Winter v. *Director of Public Prosecutions* [2003] RTR 14 – a 'City Bug' electrical trike was apprehended by a police officer. The driver admitted that she had no insurance, but claimed that it was exempt from such requirements by virtue of the Electrically Assisted Pedal Cycles Regulations 1983, SI 1983/1168. The City Bug had tiny pedals which could operate its front wheel in the manner used for the propulsion of children's tricycles. She was convicted at first instance under RTA 1988, s.143. Her appeal was dismissed by the Court of Appeal. This was a vehicle with 1-inch wide pedals, which made it very difficult to propel the vehicle by use of the pedals alone. It was intended primarily to be powered by an electric motor. Parliament's intention was that the pedals on an electrically assisted pedal cycle should be capable of propelling the vehicle in a safe manner in its normal day-to-day use. There was a finding of fact that it would be impossible for anyone to use the City Bug safely on the road if reliance were placed on the pedals alone.

6.6 'KNOWLEDGE' OF NO INSURANCE

In **Chapter 2** we considered the operation of clause 6(1)(e), (2), (3) and (4) of the 1999 Uninsured Drivers' Agreement and in **Chapter 3**, the operation of clause 5(1)(c) and (2) of the 2003 Untraced Drivers' Agreement. Briefly, these clauses state that, where the claimant knew, or ought to have known, that the vehicle had been stolen, uninsured, used for the purposes of a crime or to escape from lawful apprehension, the MIB will not be liable to pay compensation. The following cases concern present and past Uninsured Drivers' Agreements rather than the Untraced Drivers' Agreements, but it is submitted that the legal principles set out by the courts will apply to both equally.

Before *White* v. *White* below, the courts followed the strict wording of the Uninsured Drivers' Agreement. Examples are *Hadfield* v. *Knowles* (unreported, 19 September 1993), *Stinton* v. *Stinton* [1995] RTR 157 and *Clampin* v. *Palmer* [2000] *Current Law*, December, 329. Practitioners should note that the issue of knowledge is one for the Bureau to prove, rather than the other way round and that the definition of 'knowledge' following *White* v. *White* is far more restrictive than that set out in the MIB Agreements.

White v. *White* [2001] UKHL 9 – the House of Lords interpreted the MIB Agreement in line with the Second Motor Insurance Directive. In the context of art.1(4) of that Directive (now art.10(2) of the Sixth Directive) 'knew' meant primarily possession of information leading to the conclusion that the driver was uninsured. That it included the situation where the passenger possessed information leading to the conclusion that the driver might well not be insured but deliberately refrained from asking but did not extend to the situation where the passenger did not think about insurance, although an ordinary prudent passenger in his position and with his knowledge would have enquired about it. The judge's finding was no more than a finding of carelessness in that sense and therefore the claimant's claim fell outside the exclusion in the Directive. The 1988 Agreement had been entered into to give effect to the Directive and 'knew or ought to have known' in clause 6(1)(e) was intended to be co-extensive with the exclusion in art.1(4) of the Directive and to bear the same meaning as 'knew'. Accordingly, it was not apt to include mere carelessness or negligence and the MIB were not exempted from liability.

At **5.3** we considered the case of *Candolin* v. *Vahinkovakuutusosakeyhtiö Pohjola* (Case C-537/03) [2006] RTR 1 which concerned passengers who were intoxicated. In that case, the ECJ said that Member States were not permitted to include in their national legislation any exclusions from the passenger's right to compensation arising from compulsory insurance against civil liability in respect of the use of motor vehicles other than the exclusions referred to in the Directives. Consequently, the reference in clause 6(4) of the 1999 Uninsured Drivers' Agreement to the intoxication of a claimant is arguably at odds with those Directives.

The Revised Notes for Guidance to the 1999 Agreement mention the case of *White* v. *White* as being interpretative of the definition of 'knowledge' but, for all practical purposes, the effect of the case is essentially to replace the wording of clause 6(1)(e), (2), (3) and (4) of the 1999 Uninsured Drivers' Agreement with the short definition of knowledge contained in the Second Motor Insurance Directive. Practitioners are advised to read the judgment (and those below) carefully before advising a potential claimant.

Akers v. *Motor Insurers' Bureau* [2003] EWCA Civ 18 – Graham Akers, a 16-year-old, was killed in an accident. He had been one of a number of passengers in an uninsured car being driven by Mr Thorne, who was subsequently convicted of causing death by dangerous driving. Mr Thorne gave evidence to the effect that Mr Akers had heard him saying that he had no insurance. This was confirmed by another witness. However, the trial judge found that Mr Akers did not know of the absence of insurance. The Court of Appeal allowed the MIB's appeal. It said that a mere failure to make enquiries as to insurance, however negligent in the circumstances, was not enough by itself to bring the exception into play. It would apply, however, either if the passenger had actual knowledge of the lack of insurance or if he had information from which he realised that the driver might well not be insured but he deliberately refrained from asking questions lest his suspicions be confirmed.

Pickett v. *Motor Insurers' Bureau* [2004] EWCA Civ 6 – the claimant was rendered paraplegic in an accident. The car in which she was a passenger was crashed by her boyfriend. It was the property of the claimant and was uninsured and her boyfriend had no driving licence. She made a claim against her boyfriend and the MIB. She gave evidence to the effect that shortly before the accident occurred, she had asked her boyfriend to let her out of the car because of his dangerous driving. The Court of Appeal said that the elements of 'consent' and 'knowledge' did not have to happen at different times. In other words, a person could consent to getting into a car, but withdraw that consent later. Ms Pickett had not withdrawn that consent. The protest had to go beyond an objection to the manner of driving, and amount to an unequivocal repudiation of the common venture to which consent had been given when the protestor entered the vehicle.

Phillips (as Representative of the Estate of Neville Phillips Deceased) and Rafiq (1) and the Motor Insurers' Bureau (2) [2007] EWCA Civ 74 – Mr Phillips was a passenger in a vehicle driven by a Mr Rafiq, who fell asleep at the wheel. Mr Phillips was killed along with the two other passengers while Mr Rafiq survived and was convicted of driving without due care and attention. The trial judge had found that Mr Phillips knew, or ought to have known, that there was no insurance on the car. There was no appeal against that finding. Mr Phillips' spouse brought a claim against the MIB under the Fatal Accidents Act 1976 (i.e. a claim for dependency) but deliberately omitted to make a claim under the Law Reform (Miscellaneous

Provisions) Act 1934 (a claim for the benefit of Mr Phillips' estate). She argued that clause 6(1)(e) of the 1999 Uninsured Drivers' Agreement did not apply to her claim because she was not a passenger in the car, nor would the issue of 'knowledge' that there was no insurance apply. There had been a change in the wording relating to persons eligible to make claims against the MIB from the 1988 to the 1999 Uninsured Drivers' Agreement. The 1988 Agreement would have prevented her from making a claim in a fatal accident case, whereas the 1999 Agreement appeared to allow a person in her position (making a claim for dependency) to make such a claim. The Court of Appeal said that a reasonable man could not confidently say that the purpose of this Agreement was to exclude a dependant's claim. In those circumstances, the literal meaning must prevail. Consequently the claimant was able to recover as against the MIB.

Delaney v. *Pickett and another* [2011] EWCA Civ 1532 – the claimant was injured while travelling as a front-seat passenger in a car driven by the first defendant, whose insurance company relied on clause 6(1)(e)(iii) of the 1999 Agreement and claimed that the vehicle was being driven in the course of, or in furtherance of, crime. It was alleged that the claimant and the first defendant intended to travel together to acquire a sufficient quantity of cannabis for subsequent resale. The trial judge had found that the claimant 'knew' of the illegal purpose of the journey. A majority of the Court of Appeal upheld that finding.

6.7 IDENTIFYING THE DEFENDANT

Practitioners are often faced with the problem of identifying the driver involved in an incident giving rise to a claim. The Motor Insurance Database (see **Chapter 1**) enables the practitioner to match a vehicle registration number with an insurer. However, that practitioner is often then met with the assertion that the number plates have been cloned, that the registered owner of the vehicle sold it shortly before the accident, or that it was stolen by an untraced person. The insurer or the Bureau may be unable to obtain any co-operation from the likely owner or driver of the car, which only adds to the confusion as to who was driving it at the material time. Practitioners should never accept either the Bureau's or an insurer's assertion that a driver is unidentified without thorough investigation. Practitioners also need to bear in mind the way in which the courts have distinguished between an uninsured and untraced driver, together with other case law that indicates that liability for a road traffic accident can attach not only to the driver, but also possibly to a passenger or an owner of a vehicle.

In *Gurtner* v. *Circuit* [1968] 1 All ER 328, the claimant had been knocked down by a motorist who gave his details to the police and the number of a policy or cover note which was described as being 'with Lloyd's'. When enquiries were made to trace the motorist, it was found that he had emigrated to Canada, leaving no forwarding address. A writ had by this time been issued and the MIB notified, but it was unable to trace the insurers. The Court of Appeal allowed for substituted service on the Bureau and for the Bureau to be added as second defendant. It also commented that where it is not possible to ascertain the details of the insurers, the court might make an order for service at the address of the MIB. However, such an order should not be made except on evidence that all reasonable efforts have been made by the claimant to trace the defendant and effect personal service.

By contrast, in *Clarke and another* v. *Vedel and another* [1979] RTR 26, the defendant gave his name as David Vedel. He then disappeared and could not be traced. He had given a false address and no insurance details to the police. The motorcycle which he was driving was stolen and carried false number plates. There was no record of this person on the Register of Births and Deaths. The Court of Appeal said that the general principle applicable in making orders for substituted service was that the effect of the order was that it was likely that the writ would reach the defendant. In road traffic cases, there might be exceptions where a defendant could be ordered to be served at the address of his insurers or the MIB if he could not be traced and was unlikely to be reached by any form of substituted service.

It is submitted that the effect of these two cases is that, even if an identified driver disappears following an accident and cannot be traced, the court will allow alternative service on the Bureau provided it can be established that the driver was a genuine person. The Bureau does not always take the same view and may direct the practitioner to apply under the Untraced Drivers' Agreement, but this ignores the effect of *Gurtner*. Practitioners are also advised to locate the uninsured defendant as early as possible, to guard against the possibility that it cannot be established that he or she was in fact untraced. The Bureau commissions its own investigations into the whereabouts of a driver, but it would be most unwise for a practitioner to rely on its report and fail to carry out any investigation him/herself.

It is absolutely essential that practitioners ensure that the uninsured defendant is properly served with proceedings. Case law is littered with reports of service being attempted shortly before the four-month expiry period of a claim form, often with disastrous results. (See *Mather* v. *Adesuyi and the Motor Insurers' Bureau* [1995] PIQR P 454 and *Smith* v. *Hughes* [2003] EWCA Civ 656.) Practitioners should also seriously consider the use of personal service in all but the clearest of cases where the whereabouts of the defendant are beyond any doubt. They should also study the stringent requirements for notifying the MIB that service has been effected (see **Chapter 2**), and the requirements for valid service contained within rule 6 of the Civil Procedure Rules.

Where there is any doubt whether a party is traced or untraced, the prudent course is for the practitioner to make an application under both the Uninsured and Untraced Drivers' Agreements. Paragraph 11.2 of the Notes for Guidance to the 1999 Agreement states:

> In those cases where it is unclear whether the owner or driver of a vehicle has been correctly identified it is sensible for the claimant to register a claim under both this Agreement and the Untraced Drivers' Agreement following which MIB will advise which Agreement will, in its view, apply in the circumstances of the particular case.

There are, in addition, a number of cases demonstrating how a claimant can target parties other than the apparent driver. The following is a selection.

Barnard v. *Sully* (1931) 47 TLR 557 – the court held that there was a presumption that the owner of a car was the driver at the time of the accident, or that the person driving the car was that owner's servant or agent.

Monk v. *Warbey and others* [1934] All ER 373 – the Court of Appeal held that a person injured as a result of a breach of the relevant statutory provisions had a *prima facie* right to recover damages from the person breaking those provisions. The owner of the vehicle had lent it to a person who was not insured for third party risks. In permitting such use, the owner was in breach of what is now re-enacted as RTA 1988, s.143(1). The claimant was awarded damages against the owner on the basis that he had permitted the uninsured use of the vehicle.

Scarsbrook and others v. *Mason* [1961] 3 All ER 767 – the claimants were injured while standing on a footpath when a car was driven so fast round a bend that the driver lost control of it and knocked them down. A jacket belonging to the defendant had been found after the incident, caught in the offside rear door of the car. He stated that he had accepted the invitation of the other occupant of the car to go for a ride and had paid four shillings as a contribution towards petrol. His evidence was that he was not the driver of the car and he did not know who the driver was. The judge held that the occupants were:

> ... jointly and severally liable for the manner in which the motor car was driven, *viz*, that it was driven negligently and the plaintiffs were entitled to succeed against this member of the party on the ground that the driver was acting as agent for each and all the members of that party.

This principle also applies when the persons using the vehicle are doing so in pursuance of some joint unlawful purpose.

Roger v. *Riders (a firm)* [1983] RTR 324 – a minicab firm was held by the Court of Appeal to be under a duty to ensure not only that it provided cars properly maintained and reasonably fit for the purpose of conveying customers safely to their destinations, but also to provide drivers fit for that purpose. During the claimant's journey, a side door flew open, hit a stationary vehicle and rebounded, hitting the claimant. The driver could not be traced and an action against him was discontinued. The minicab firm was held liable on the basis that the vehicle was defective, and the firm was in breach of its duty to take reasonable steps to ensure that the vehicle was properly maintained and reasonably fit for the stated purpose. That duty could not be delegated to the driver, whether he was an employee or an independent contractor.

Pask and another v. *Keefe and another* (Webster J in the Queen's Bench Division on 25 April 1985) – ownership of a vehicle is *prima facie* evidence that it was being driven at the material time by such an owner or his servant or agent. Although it was not conclusively proved that the defendant was the driver of the taxi, judgment was nevertheless entered against the owner of the taxi.

6.8   CONFLICTS BETWEEN THE UNTRACED DRIVERS' AGREEMENT AND THE SECOND MOTOR INSURANCE DIRECTIVE

As we have seen in all the chapters throughout this book, the European Motor Insurance Directives play a crucial part in the interpretation of the Bureau's Agreements and motor insurance law in general. In some cases they have led to major changes in the Agreements. The prime example of a case effecting such a change is that of *Evans* v. *Secretary of State for the Environment, Transport and Regions and the Motor Insurers' Bureau* (Case C-63/01), which concerned the 1972 Untraced Drivers' Agreement.

Mr Evans was injured in 1991 by an untraced vehicle. He made a claim under the Untraced Drivers' Agreement and an award was made by the MIB. Mr Evans then appealed to the arbitrator, who awarded a lesser sum after making a deduction for contributory negligence. Mr Evans then obtained leave to appeal from the arbitrator's decision, but lost in the court of first instance. He subsequently appealed to the Court of Appeal, where his case was determined alongside two other cases which concerned the definition of 'knowledge' under clause 6(1) of the 1988 Uninsured Drivers' Agreement as opposed to that found in the Second Motor Insurance Directive.

The Court of Appeal said that the Second Motor Insurance Directive was not of direct effect and consequently Mr Evans could not rely on it. Furthermore, while national courts were under a duty to interpret national law in conformity with European Community law, that principle did not extend to the Untraced Drivers' Agreement, which was an agreement between a Member State and another person. Mr Evans was refused leave to appeal to the House of Lords.

Consequently, Mr Evans launched a '*Francovich*' action (*Francovich* v. *Italian Republic* (Cases C-6/90 and C-9/90) [1991] ECR I-5357) against both the Secretary of State and the MIB, who were the parties to the 1972 Untraced Drivers' Agreement. He alleged that the UK government had failed to implement the Second Motor Insurance Directive. If the Directive had been properly implemented, he claimed, he would have received a higher award, as well as interest and costs. The case was referred to the ECJ to decide:

(a)   whether the MIB was duly authorised by the Secretary of State, pursuant to the Directive;

(b)   whether the Secretary of State was in breach of his obligations under the Directive in respect of:

    (i)   the absence of any provision for the payment of interest;

    (ii)   the absence of any provision for the payment of costs;

(iii) the procedural method adopted by the MIB in relation to claims by victims of unidentified drivers;

(c) in the event that the answers to any of the above questions was 'yes', whether the claimant was a member of a class of persons intended to be protected or benefited by the Directive and thereby entitled to bring an action against the Secretary of State.

The ECJ held that the procedural arrangements laid down under the 1972 Untraced Drivers' Agreement did not render it practically impossible or excessively difficult to exercise the right to compensation conferred on victims for damage or injury caused by unidentified or insufficiently insured vehicles. Nevertheless, the procedure had to guarantee that, both in dealing with the MIB and before the arbitrator, victims were made aware of any matter that might be used against them and that they be given the opportunity to submit their comments thereon. It would be for the national court to determine whether those conditions had been fulfilled in Mr Evans' case.

In relation to interest, the ECJ said that compensation for loss could not leave out of account factors such as the effluxion of time. In relation to costs, the court said that the MIB's Agreement was not required to include reimbursement of costs, except to the extent that such reimbursement was necessary to safeguard the rights derived under the Directive in conformity with the principles of equivalence and effectiveness. Again, it was for the national court to consider whether that was the case under the procedural arrangements adopted in the Member State concerned.

As to whether Mr Evans was of a class of person affected by the breach of the Directive, the court commented that, even if the MIB was not sufficiently authorised to deal with his claim under the Directive, he would have suffered no loss. Any other issues were for the national courts to decide.

Mr Evans' case was remitted back to the High Court and judgment was given by Judge Mackie QC in *Evans* v. *Secretary of State for the Environment, Transport and the Regions and another* [2006] EWHC 322 (QB). By that time, the defendants had made an open offer and defended the claim on the basis that Mr Evans could not hope to achieve a better result if he went forward with his claim. Judge Mackie said that Mr Evans had no real prospect of success in establishing any of his claims for damages with the exception of those relating to his legal fees for making the application and appealing to the arbitrator and as regards interest on the award. However, those claims would not have exceeded the open offer made by the defendants, and, consequently, continuation of the case could not be permitted. Although Mr Evans lost his case, he achieved a major step forward for other victims of untraced drivers because as a result of his litigation, the government and the Bureau introduced the current Untraced Drivers' Agreement in 2003. This Agreement tries to meet the defects of the former Agreements by providing for interest to be paid and for some limited costs as well introducing a much improved appeal procedure.

A similar challenge was made to the 1972 Untraced Drivers' Agreement in *Moore* v. *Secretary of State for Transport and Motor Insurers' Bureau* [2008] EWCA Civ 750. The issue before the Court of Appeal was the limitation period for a *Francovich* action. Mr Moore had been injured in 1995, but only issued his *Francovich* action against the Secretary of State and the MIB in 2006. The Court of Appeal determined that the time limit for such an action was statute barred by the six-year period under the Limitation Act 1980, s.2.

In *Byrne (a Minor)* v. *The Motor Insurers' Bureau and the Secretary of State for Transport* [2008] EWCA Civ 574, the claimant had been born in 1989. At the age of three, he was injured by an untraced driver. His parents did not obtain legal advice and were unaware of the existence of the MIB. However, they first became aware of the possibility of making a claim in October 2001. Their application was rejected by the MIB relying on clause 1(1)(f) of the 1972 Untraced Drivers' Agreement, which stated that applications must be brought within three years of the accident. The Court of Appeal considered the judgment of the ECJ in *Evans* and said that the MIB procedure should be subject to a limitation period no less favourable than that which applied under the Limitation Act 1980. It was this case that led to the 2008 Supplementary Agreement. There is also a Memorandum of Understanding published on the MIB's website, setting out how it proposes to deal with pre-*Byrne* cases.

6.9 OIL SPILLS OR DEBRIS ON THE ROAD

Where a motorist's vehicle slips on oil on the road, it may be possible to make a claim on the MIB under the 2003 Untraced Drivers' Agreement on the basis that the accident was caused by the 'use' of an untraced vehicle, i.e. the vehicle that spilt the oil. A claim can also be made under the 2003 Agreement not only for fuel spills but also debris on the road, or being blinded by headlights. The possibility of making such a claim is discussed in an article by Andrew Campbell of Withy King in the *Journal of Personal Injury Law*, issue 2/07. See also *Conti* v. *Hugh James (a firm)* (2003) *APIL PI Focus*, vol. 14, issue 4 where a claim in professional negligence was made against a firm which had failed to consider making a claim to the Bureau for a spill on the road.

6.10 RE-ISSUE OF PROCEEDINGS

One of the major problems for practitioners when dealing with the Bureau in uninsured driver cases is the need to comply with the draconian provisions of the 1999 Agreement. As we saw in **Chapter 1**, the introduction of that Agreement was widely criticised because any kind of failure (however minor) to comply with those provisions can lead to the refusal of the claim. This is a particular problem where proceedings have been issued but the limitation period has passed. The Bureau may then point to some non-compliance on the part of the claimant and refuse to make an award. The 1999 Agreement makes it very clear that the Bureau is entitled to take this stance.

If the claim is issued well before limitation, this is not so much of a problem because the claimant need only abandon his or her proceedings and re-issue, so as to comply with the strict terms of the Agreement. *O'Neill* v. *O'Brien and another* (Times Law Reports, 21 March 1997, CA) confirmed that a second action would be allowed by the court if there was non-compliance with the MIB Agreement. However, before *Horton* v. *Sadler and another* [2006] UKHL 27, any non-compliance with the provisions of the Uninsured Drivers' Agreement after the expiry of limitation would have disastrous results, because the court would not allow re-issue. In *Silverton* v. *Goodall and the Motor Insurers' Bureau* [1997] PIQR P 451, the claimant's solicitors served their notice of issue 15 days later, because they did not receive the notice from the court until after the seven-day time limit had expired. The Bureau refused to pay the claim. Its decision was upheld by the court. This is a major problem at present in the county court system, as there are considerable delays reported from the processing centres which issue the claims.

It is possible for the Bureau to waive its right to rely on the seven-day notice period. In *Begum* v. *Ullah* [1998] *Current Law* 590, the claimant's solicitor was aware that she had failed to comply with the seven-day time limit for giving notice. She had a telephone conversation with the MIB in which she asked it to waive the time limit to avoid the need for re-issue. This was said to have been agreed, but the MIB later refused to pay out because it said that it had received no proper notice. The court found that the MIB was estopped from raising the point.

The House of Lords decision in *Horton* v. *Sadler* provided much-needed assistance to practitioners faced with this problem. The claimant's solicitors issued within the limitation period, but failed to notify the Bureau in accordance with the 1988 Uninsured Drivers' Agreement. Around five months after limitation, they re-issued proceedings. The court at first instance indicated that it would have applied s.33 of the Limitation Act 1980 in the claimant's favour, but applying the doctrine in *Walkley* v. *Precision Forgings Ltd* [1979] 1 WLR 606, the claim was struck out. The House of Lords said that re-issue of the proceedings outside the limitation period was not necessarily an abuse of process, and applied s.33 in the claimant's favour. *Horton* v. *Sadler* was followed in later cases: *Richardson* v. *Watson and another* [2006] EWCA Civ 1662 and *Cain* v. *Francis; McKay* v. *Hamlani* and another [2008] EWCA Civ 1451.

However, practitioners should note that the court is not always prepared to exercise discretion in the claimant's favour. See *McDonnell and another* v. *Walker* [2009] EWCA Civ 1257 and *Williams* v. *Johnstone* [2008] All ER (D) 32 (May). Consequently, the prudent course in any case involving the Bureau (or an insurer for that matter) is to issue proceedings well within the limitation period so as to leave room to re-issue if there has been some non-compliance with the Agreement.

The 1999 Uninsured Drivers' Agreement

AGREEMENT

THIS AGREEMENT is made the thirteenth day of August 1999 between the SECRETARY OF STATE FOR THE ENVIRONMENT, TRANSPORT AND THE REGIONS (hereinafter referred to as 'the Secretary of State') and the MOTOR INSURERS' BUREAU, whose registered office is at 152 Silbury Boulevard, Milton Keynes MK9 1NB (hereinafter referred to as 'MIB') and is SUPPLEMENTAL to an Agreement (hereinafter called 'the Principal Agreement') made the 31st Day of December 1945 between the Minister of War Transport and the insurers transacting compulsory motor insurance business in Great Britain by or on behalf of whom the said Agreement was signed and in pursuance of paragraph 1 of which MIB was incorporated.

IT IS HEREBY AGREED AS FOLLOWS:

INTERPRETATION

General definitions

1. In this Agreement, unless the context otherwise requires, the following expressions have the following meanings –

    '1988 Act' means the Road Traffic Act 1988;

    '1988 Agreement' means the Agreement made on 21 December 1988 between the Secretary of State for Transport and MIB;

    'bank holiday' means a day which is, or is to be observed as, a bank holiday under the Banking and Financial Dealings Act 1971;

    'claimant' means a person who has commenced or who proposes to commence relevant proceedings and has made an application under this Agreement in respect thereof;

    'contract of insurance' means a policy of insurance or a security covering a relevant liability;

    'insurer' includes the giver of a security;

    'MIB's obligation' means the obligation contained in clause 5;

    'property' means any property whether real, heritable or personal;

    'relevant liability' means a liability in respect of which a contract of insurance must be in force to comply with Part VI of the 1988 Act;

    'relevant proceedings' means proceedings in respect of a relevant liability (and 'commencement', in relation to such proceedings means, in England and Wales, the date on which a Claim Form or other originating process is issued by a Court or, in Scotland, the date on which the originating process is served on the Defender);

'relevant sum' means a sum payable or remaining payable under an unsatisfied judgment, including –

(a) an amount payable or remaining payable in respect of interest on that sum, and

(b) either the whole of the costs (whether taxed or not) awarded by the Court as part of that judgment or, where the judgment includes an award in respect of a liability which is not a relevant liability, such proportion of those costs as the relevant liability bears to the total sum awarded under the judgment;

'specified excess' means £300 or such other sum as may from time to time be agreed in writing between the Secretary of State and MIB;

'unsatisfied judgment' means a judgment or order (by whatever name called) in respect of a relevant liability which has not been satisfied in full within seven days from the date upon which the claimant became entitled to enforce it.

Meaning of references

2. (1) Save as otherwise herein provided, the Interpretation Act 1978 shall apply for the interpretation of this Agreement as it applies for the interpretation of an Act of Parliament.

(2) Where, under this Agreement, something is required to be done –

(a) within a specified period after or from the happening of a particular event, the period begins on the day after the happening of that event;

(b) within or not less than a specified period before a particular event, the period ends on the day immediately before the happening of that event.

(3) Where, apart from this paragraph, the period in question, being a period of seven days or less, would include a Saturday, Sunday or bank holiday or Christmas Day or Good Friday, that day shall be excluded.

(4) Save where expressly otherwise provided, a reference in this Agreement to a numbered clause is a reference to the clause bearing that number in this Agreement and a reference to a numbered paragraph is a reference to a paragraph bearing that number in the clause in which the reference occurs.

(5) In this Agreement –

(a) a reference (however framed) to the doing of any act or thing by or the happening of any event in relation to the claimant includes a reference to the doing of that act or thing by or the happening of that event in relation to a Solicitor or other person acting on his behalf, and

(b) a requirement to give notice to, or to serve documents upon, MIB or an insurer mentioned in clause 9(1)(a) shall be satisfied by the giving of the notice to, or the service of the documents upon, a Solicitor acting on its behalf in the manner provided for.

Claimants not of full age or capacity

3. Where, under and in accordance with this Agreement –

(a) any act or thing is done to or by a Solicitor or other person acting on behalf of a claimant,

(b) any decision is made by or in respect of a Solicitor or other person acting on behalf of a claimant, or

(c) any sum is paid to a Solicitor or other person acting on behalf of a claimant, then, whatever may be the age or other circumstances affecting the capacity of the claimant, that act, thing, decision or sum shall be treated as if it had been done to or by, or made in respect of or paid to a claimant of full age and capacity.

PRINCIPAL TERMS

Duration of Agreement

4. (1) This Agreement shall come into force on 1st October 1999 in relation to accidents occurring on or after that date and, save as provided by clause 23, the 1988 Agreement shall cease and determine immediately before that date.

    (2) This Agreement may be determined by the Secretary of State or by MIB giving to the other not less than twelve months' notice in writing but without prejudice to its continued operation in respect of accidents occurring before the date of termination.

MIB's obligation to satisfy compensation claims

5. (1) Subject to clauses 6 to 17, if a claimant has obtained against any person in a Court in Great Britain a judgment which is an unsatisfied judgment then MIB will pay the relevant sum to, or to the satisfaction of, the claimant or will cause the same to be so paid.

    (2) Paragraph (1) applies whether or not the person liable to satisfy the judgment is in fact covered by a contract of insurance and whatever may be the cause of his failure to satisfy the judgment.

EXCEPTIONS TO AGREEMENT

6. (1) Clause 5 does not apply in the case of an application made in respect of a claim of any of the following descriptions (and, where part only of a claim satisfies such a description, clause 5 does not apply to that part) –

    (a) a claim arising out of a relevant liability incurred by the user of a vehicle owned by or in the possession of the Crown, unless –

        (i) responsibility for the existence of a contract of insurance under Part VI of the 1988 Act in relation to that vehicle had been undertaken by some other person (whether or not the person liable was in fact covered by a contract of insurance), or

        (ii) the relevant liability was in fact covered by a contract of insurance;

    (b) a claim arising out of the use of a vehicle which is not required to be covered by a contract of insurance by virtue of section 144 of the 1988 Act, unless the use is in fact covered by such a contract;

    (c) a claim by, or for the benefit of, a person ('the beneficiary') other than the person suffering death, injury or other damage which is made either –

        (i) in respect of a cause of action or a judgment which has been assigned to the beneficiary, or

        (ii) pursuant to a right of subrogation or contractual or other right belonging to the beneficiary;

    (d) a claim in respect of damage to a motor vehicle or losses arising therefrom where, at the time when the damage to it was sustained –

      (i)   there was not in force in relation to the use of that vehicle such a contract of insurance as is required by Part VI of the 1988 Act, and

      (ii)   the claimant either knew or ought to have known that that was the case;

(e)   a claim which is made in respect of a relevant liability described in paragraph (2) by a claimant who, at the time of the use giving rise to the relevant liability was voluntarily allowing himself to be carried in the vehicle and, either before the commencement of his journey in the vehicle or after such commencement if he could reasonably be expected to have alighted from it, knew or ought to have known that –

      (i)   the vehicle had been stolen or unlawfully taken,

      (ii)   the vehicle was being used without there being in force in relation to its use such a contract of insurance as would comply with Part VI of the 1988 Act,

      (iii)   the vehicle was being used in the course or furtherance of a crime, or

      (iv)   the vehicle was being used as a means of escape from, or avoidance of, lawful apprehension.

(2)   The relevant liability referred to in paragraph (1)(e) is a liability incurred by the owner or registered keeper or a person using the vehicle in which the claimant was being carried.

(3)   The burden of proving that the claimant knew or ought to have known of any matter set out in paragraph (1)(e) shall be on MIB but, in the absence of evidence to the contrary, proof by MIB of any of the following matters shall be taken as proof of the claimant's knowledge of the matter set out in paragraph (1)(e)(ii) –

(a)   that the claimant was the owner or registered keeper of the vehicle or had caused or permitted its use;

(b)   that the claimant knew the vehicle was being used by a person who was below the minimum age at which he could be granted a licence authorising the driving of a vehicle of that class;

(c)   that the claimant knew that the person driving the vehicle was disqualified for holding or obtaining a driving licence;

(d)   that the claimant knew that the user of the vehicle was neither its owner nor registered keeper nor an employee of the owner or registered keeper nor the owner or registered keeper of any other vehicle.

(4)   Knowledge which the claimant has or ought to have for the purposes of paragraph (1)(e) includes knowledge of matters which he could reasonably be expected to have been aware of had he not been under the self-induced influence of drink or drugs.

(5)   For the purposes of this clause –

(a)   a vehicle which has been unlawfully removed from the possession of the Crown shall be taken to continue in that possession whilst it is kept so removed,

(b)   references to a person being carried in a vehicle include references to his being carried upon, entering, getting on to and alighting from the vehicle, and

(c)   'owner', in relation to a vehicle which is the subject of a hiring agreement or a hire-purchase agreement, means the person in possession of the vehicle under that agreement.

CONDITIONS PRECEDENT TO MIB'S OBLIGATION

Form of application

7.   (1)   MIB shall incur no liability under MIB's obligation unless an application is made to the person specified in clause 9(1) –

      (a)   in such form,

      (b)   giving such information about the relevant proceedings and other matters relevant to this Agreement, and

      (c)   accompanied by such documents as MIB may reasonably require.

   (2)   Where an application is signed by a person who is neither the claimant nor a Solicitor acting on his behalf MIB may refuse to accept the application (and shall incur no liability under MIB's obligation) until it is reasonably satisfied that, having regard to the status of the signatory and his relationship to the claimant, the claimant is fully aware of the contents and effect of the application but subject thereto MIB shall not refuse to accept such an application by reason only that it is signed by a person other than the claimant or his Solicitor.

Service of notices etc.

8.   Any notice required to be given or documents to be supplied to MIB pursuant to clauses 9 to 12 of this Agreement shall be sufficiently given or supplied only if sent by facsimile transmission or by Registered or Recorded Delivery post to MIB's registered office for the time being and delivery shall be proved by the production of a facsimile transmission report produced by the sender's facsimile machine or an appropriate postal receipt.

Notice of relevant proceedings

9.   (1)   MIB shall incur no liability under MIB's obligation unless proper notice of the bringing of the relevant proceedings has been given by the claimant not later than fourteen days after the commencement of those proceedings –

      (a)   in the case of proceedings in respect of a relevant liability which is covered by a contract of insurance with an insurer whose identity can be ascertained, to that insurer;

      (b)   in any other case, to MIB.

   (2)   In this clause 'proper notice' means, except in so far as any part of such information or any copy document or other thing has already been supplied under clause 7 –

      (a)   notice in writing that proceedings have been commenced by Claim Form, Writ, or other means,

      (b)   a copy of the sealed Claim Form, Writ or other official document providing evidence of the commencement of the proceedings and, in Scotland, a statement of the means of service,

      (c)   a copy or details of any insurance policy providing benefits in the case of the death, bodily injury or damage to property to which the proceedings relate where the claimant is the insured party and the benefits are available to him,

      (d)   copies of all correspondence in the possession of the claimant or (as the case may be) his Solicitor or agent to or from the Defendant or the Defender or (as the case may be) his Solicitor, insurers or agent which is relevant to –

         (i)   the death, bodily injury or damage for which the Defendant or Defender is alleged to be responsible, or

> (ii) any contract of insurance which covers, or which may or has been alleged to cover, liability for such death, injury or damage the benefit of which is, or is claimed to be, available to Defendant or Defender,
>
> (e) subject to paragraph (3), a copy of the Particulars of Claim whether or not indorsed on the Claim Form, Writ or other originating process, and whether or not served (in England and Wales) on any Defendant or (in Scotland) on any Defender, and
>
> (f) a copy of all other documents which are required under the appropriate rules of procedure to be served on a Defendant or Defender with the Claim Form, Writ or other originating process or with the Particulars of Claim,
>
> (g) such other information about the relevant proceedings as MIB may reasonably specify.

(3) If, in the case of proceedings commenced in England or Wales, the Particulars of Claim (including any document required to be served therewith) has not yet been served with the Claim Form or other originating process paragraph (2)(e) shall be sufficiently complied with if a copy thereof is served on MIB not later than seven days after it is served on the Defendant.

Notice of service of proceedings

10. (1) This clause applies where the relevant proceedings are commenced in England or Wales.

(2) MIB shall incur no liability under MIB's obligation unless the claimant has, not later than the appropriate date, given notice in writing to the person specified in clause 9(1) of the date of service of the Claim Form or other originating process in the relevant proceedings.

(3) In this clause, 'the appropriate date' means the day falling –

> (a) seven days after –
>
> > (i) the date when the claimant receives notification from the Court that service of the Claim Form or other originating process has occurred,
> >
> > (ii) the date when the claimant receives notification from the Defendant that service of the Claim Form or other originating process has occurred, or
> >
> > (iii) the date of personal service, or
>
> (b) fourteen days after the date when service is deemed to have occurred in accordance with the Civil Procedure Rules,

whichever of those days occurs first.

Further information

11. (1) MIB shall incur no liability under MIB's obligation unless the claimant has, not later than seven days after the occurrence of any of the following events, namely –

> (a) the filing of a defence in the relevant proceedings,
>
> (b) any amendment to the Particulars of Claim or any amendment of or addition to any schedule or other document required to be served therewith, and
>
> (c) either –
>
> > (i) the setting down of the case for trial, or
> >
> > (ii) where the court gives notice to the claimant of the trial date, the date when that notice is received,

given notice in writing of the date of that event to the person specified in clause 9(1) and has, in the case of the filing of a defence or an amendment of the Particulars of Claim or any amendment of or addition to any schedule or other document required to be served therewith, supplied a copy thereof to that person.

(2) MIB shall incur no liability under MIB's obligation unless the claimant furnishes to the person specified in clause 9(1) within a reasonable time after being required to do so such further information and documents in support of his claim as MIB may reasonably require notwithstanding that the claimant may have complied with clause 7(1).

Notice of intention to apply for judgment

12. (1) MIB shall incur no liability under MIB's obligation unless the claimant has, after commencement of the relevant proceedings and not less than thirty-five days before the appropriate date, given notice in writing to the person specified in clause 9(1) of his intention to apply for or to sign judgment in the relevant proceedings.

(2) In this clause, 'the appropriate date' means the date when the application for judgment is made or, as the case may be, the signing of judgment occurs.

Section 154 of the 1988 Act

13. MIB shall incur no liability under MIB's obligation unless the claimant has as soon as reasonably practicable –

(a) demanded the information and, where appropriate, the particulars specified in section 154(1) of the 1988 Act, and

(b) if the person of whom the demand is made fails to comply with the provisions of that subsection –

    (i) made a formal complaint to a police officer in respect of such failure, and

    (ii) used all reasonable endeavours to obtain the name and address of the registered keeper of the vehicle,

or, if so required by MIB, has authorised MIB to take such steps on his behalf.

Prosecution of proceedings

14. MIB shall incur no liability under MIB's obligation –

(a) unless the claimant has, if so required by MIB and having been granted a full indemnity by MIB as to costs, taken all reasonable steps to obtain judgment against every person who may be liable (including any person who may be vicariously liable) in respect of the injury or death or damage to property, or

(b) if the claimant, upon being requested to do so by MIB, refuses to consent to MIB being joined as a party to the relevant proceedings.

Assignment of judgment and undertakings

15. MIB shall incur no liability under MIB's obligation unless the claimant has –

(a) assigned to MIB or its nominee the unsatisfied judgment, whether or not that judgment includes an amount in respect of a liability other than a relevant liability, and any order for costs made in the relevant proceedings, and

(b) undertaken to repay to MIB any sum paid to him –

    (i) by MIB in discharge of MIB's obligation if the judgment is subsequently set aside either as a whole or in respect of the part of the relevant liability to which that sum relates;

(ii)   by any other person by way of compensation or benefit for the death, bodily injury or other damage to which the relevant proceedings relate, including a sum which would have been deductible under the provisions of clause 17 if it had been received before MIB was obliged to satisfy MIB's obligation.

LIMITATIONS ON MIB'S LIABILITY

Compensation for damage to property

16.   (1)   Where a claim under this Agreement includes a claim in respect of damage to property, MIB's obligation in respect of that part of the relevant sum which is awarded for such damage and any losses arising therefrom (referred to in this clause as 'the property damage compensation') is limited in accordance with the following paragraphs.

(2)   Where the property damage compensation does not exceed the specified excess, MIB shall incur no liability.

(3)   Where the property damage compensation in respect of any one accident exceeds the specified excess but does not exceed £250,000, MIB shall incur liability only in respect of the property damage compensation less the specified excess.

(4)   Where the property damage compensation in respect of any one accident exceeds £250,000, MIB shall incur liability only in respect of the sum of £250,000 less the specified excess.

Compensation received from other sources

17.   Where a claimant has received compensation from –

(a)   the Policyholders Protection Board under the Policyholders Protection Act 1975, or

(b)   an insurer under an insurance agreement or arrangement, or

(c)   any other source,

in respect of the death, bodily injury or other damage to which the relevant proceedings relate and such compensation has not been taken into account in the calculation of the relevant sum MIB may deduct from the relevant sum, in addition to any sum deductible under clause 16, an amount equal to that compensation.

MISCELLANEOUS

Notifications of decisions by MIB

18.   Where a claimant –

(a)   has made an application in accordance with clause 7, and

(b)   has given to the person specified in clause 9(1) proper notice of the relevant proceedings in accordance with clause 9(2),

MIB shall –

(i)   give a reasoned reply to any request made by the claimant relating to the payment of compensation in pursuance of MIB's obligation, and

    (ii)   as soon as reasonably practicable notify the claimant in writing of its decision regarding the payment of the relevant sum, together with the reasons for that decision.

Reference of disputes to the Secretary of State

19. (1)   In the event of any dispute as to the reasonableness of a requirement made by MIB for the supply of information or documentation or for the taking of any step by the claimant, it may be referred by the claimant or MIB to the Secretary of State whose decision shall be final.

    (2)   Where a dispute is referred to the Secretary of State –

       (a)   MIB shall supply the Secretary of State and, if it has not already done so, the claimant with notice in writing of the requirement from which the dispute arises, together with the reasons for that requirement and such further information as MIB considers relevant, and

       (b)   where the dispute is referred by the claimant, the claimant shall supply the Secretary of State and, if he has not already done so, MIB with notice in writing of the grounds on which he disputes the reasonableness of the requirement.

Recoveries

20.   Nothing in this Agreement shall prevent an insurer from providing by conditions in a contract of insurance that all sums paid by the insurer or by MIB by virtue of the Principal Agreement or this Agreement in or towards the discharge of the liability of the insured shall be recoverable by them or by MIB from the insured or from any other person.

Apportionment of damages, etc.

21. (1)   Where an unsatisfied judgment which includes an amount in respect of a liability other than a relevant liability has been assigned to MIB or its nominee in pursuance of clause 15 MIB shall –

       (a)   apportion any sum it receives in satisfaction or partial satisfaction of the judgment according to the proportion which the damages awarded in respect of the relevant liability bear to the damages awarded in respect of the other liability, and

       (b)   account to the claimant in respect of the moneys received properly apportionable to the other liability.

    (2)   Where the sum received includes an amount in respect of interest or an amount awarded under an order for costs, the interest or the amount received in pursuance of the order shall be dealt with in the manner provided in paragraph (1).

Agents

22.   MIB may perform any of its obligations under this Agreement by agents.

Transitional provisions

23. (1) The 1988 Agreement shall continue in force in relation to claims arising out of accidents occurring before 1st October 1999 with the modifications contained in paragraph (2).

   (2) In relation to any claim made under the 1988 Agreement after this Agreement has come into force, the 1988 Agreement shall apply as if there were inserted after clause 6 thereof –

   > '6A. Where any person in whose favour a judgment in respect of a relevant liability has been made has –
   > (a) made a claim under this Agreement, and
   > (b) satisfied the requirements specified in clause 5 hereof,
   > MIB shall, if requested to do so, give him a reasoned reply regarding the satisfaction of that claim.'

IN WITNESS whereof the Secretary of State has caused his Corporate Seal to be hereunto affixed and the Motor Insurer's Bureau has caused its Common Seal to be hereunto affixed the day and year first above written.

THE CORPORATE SEAL of the SECRETARY OF STATE FOR THE ENVIRONMENT, TRANSPORT AND THE REGIONS hereunto affixed is authenticated by:

Richard Jones
Authorised by the Secretary of State

THE COMMON SEAL of the MOTOR INSURERS' BUREAU was hereunto affixed in the presence of:

James Arthur Read
Roger Merer Jones

Directors of the Board of Management
Byford Louisy
Secretary

NOTES FOR THE GUIDANCE OF VICTIMS OF ROAD TRAFFIC ACCIDENTS

The following notes are for the guidance of anyone who may have a claim on the Motor Insurers' Bureau under this Agreement and their legal advisers. They are not part of the Agreement, their purpose being to deal in ordinary language with the situations which most readily occur. They are not in any way a substitute for reading and applying the terms of this or any other relevant Agreement, nor are they intended to control or influence the legal interpretation of the Agreement.

At the request of the Secretary of State, these notes have been revised with effect from 15th April 2002 and in their revised form have been agreed and approved by MIB, the Law Society of England and Wales, the Law Society of Scotland, the Motor Accident Solicitors' Society and the Association of Personal Injury Lawyers. Any application made under the Agreement after this date (unless proceedings have already been issued) will be handled by MIB in accordance with these notes.

Where proceedings have been issued in Scotland, for the words 'Claimant' and 'Defendant' there shall be substituted in these Notes where appropriate the words 'Pursuer' and 'Defender' respectively.

Enquiries, requests for application forms and general correspondence in connection with the Agreement should be addressed to:

Motor Insurers' Bureau
Linford Word House
6–12 Capital Drive
Milton Keynes
MK14 6XT

Tel: 01908 830001
Fax: 01908 671681
DX: 142620 Milton Keynes

1. INTRODUCTION – MIB'S ROLE AND APPLICATION OF THE AGREEMENT

1.1   The role of MIB under this Agreement is to provide a safety net for innocent victims of drivers who have been identified but are uninsured. MIB's funds for this purpose are obtained from levies charged upon insurers and so come from the premiums which are charged by those insurers to members of the public.

1.2   MIB has entered into a series of Agreements with the Secretary of State and his predecessors in office. Under each Agreement MIB undertakes obligations to pay defined compensation in specific circumstances. There are two sets of Agreements, one relating to victims of uninsured drivers (the 'Uninsured Drivers' Agreements) and the other concerned with victims of hit and run or otherwise untraceable drivers (the 'Untraced Drivers' Agreements). These Notes are addressed specifically to the procedures required to take advantage of the rights granted by the Uninsured Drivers Agreements. However, it is not always certain which of the Agreements applies. For guidance in such cases please see the note on **Untraced Drivers** at paragraph 11 below.

1.3   In order to determine which of the Uninsured Drivers Agreements is applicable to a particular victim's claim, regard must be had to the date of the relevant accident. This Agreement only applies in respect of claims arising on or after 1st October 1999. Claims arising earlier than that are covered by the following Agreements:

1.3.1 Claims arising in respect of an incident occurring between 1st July 1946 and 28th February 1971 are governed by the Agreement between the Minister of Transport and the Bureau dated 17th June 1946.

1.3.2 Claims arising in respect of an incident occurring between 1st March 1971 and 30th November 1972 are governed by the Agreement between the Secretary of State for the Environment and the Bureau dated 1st February 1971.

1.3.3 Claims arising in respect of an incident occurring between 1st December 1972 and 30th December 1988 are governed by the Agreement between the Secretary of State and the Bureau dated 22nd November 1972.

1.3.4 Claims arising in respect of an incident occurring between 31st December 1988 and 30th September 1999 are governed by the Agreement between the Secretary of State and the Bureau dated 21st December 1988.

2. MIB'S OBLIGATION

2.1 MIB's basic obligation (see clause 5) is to satisfy judgments which fall within the terms of this Agreement and which, because the Defendant to the proceedings is not insured, are not satisfied.

2.2 This obligation is, however, not absolute. It is subject to certain exceptions where MIB has no liability (see clause 6), there are a number of pre-conditions which the claimant must comply with (see clauses 7 to 15) and there are some limitations on MIB's liability (see clauses 16 and 17).

2.3 Nothing in the Agreement is intended to vary the limitation rules applying to claimants not of full age or capacity. Limitation for personal injury remains 3 years from the date of full age or capacity.

2.4 MIB does not have to wait for a judgment to be given; it can become party to the proceedings or negotiate and settle the claim if it wishes to do so.

3. CLAIMS WHICH MIB IS NOT OBLIGED TO SATISFY

MIB is not liable under the Agreement in the case of the following types of claim.

3.1 A claim made in respect of an unsatisfied judgment which does not concern a liability against which Part VI of the Road Traffic Act 1988 requires a vehicle user to insure (see section 145 of the Act). An example would be a case where the accident did not occur in a place specified in the Act. See the definitions of 'unsatisfied judgment' and 'relevant liability' in clause 1.

3.2 A claim in respect of loss or damage caused by the use of a vehicle owned by or in the possession of the Crown (that is the Civil Service, the armed forces and so on) to which Part VI does not apply. If the responsibility for motor insurance has been undertaken by someone else or the vehicle is in fact insured, this exception does not apply. See clause 6(1)(a).

3.3 A claim made against any person who is not required to insure by virtue of section 144 of the Road Traffic Act 1988. See clause 6(1)(b).

3.4 A claim (commonly called subrogated) made in the name of a person suffering damage or injury but which is in fact wholly or partly for the benefit of another who has indemnified, or is liable to indemnify, that person. See clause 6(1)(c).

It is not the intention of this Clause to exclude claims for the gratuitous provision of care, travel expenses by family members or friends, or miscellaneous expenses incurred on behalf of the Claimant, where the claimant is entitled to include such claims in his claim for damages.

3.5 A claim in respect of damage to a motor vehicle or losses arising from such damage where the use of the damaged vehicle was itself not covered by a contract of insurance as required by law. See clause 6(1)(d).

3.6 A claim made by a passenger in a vehicle where the loss or damage has been caused by the user of that vehicle if:

3.6.1 the use of the vehicle was not covered by a contract of insurance; and

3.6.2 the claimant knew or could be taken to have known that the vehicle was being used without insurance, had been stolen or unlawfully taken or was being used in connection with crime.

See clause 6(1)(e), (2), (3) and (4).

For an interpretation of 'knew or ought to have known' refer to the House of Lords judgment in *White* v. *White* of 1st March 2001.

3.7 A claim in respect of property damage amounting to £300 or less, £300 being the 'specified excess'. See clause 16(2).

3.8 Where the claim is for property damage, the first £300 of the loss and so much of it as exceeds £250,000. See clause 16(3) and (4).

4. PROCEDURE AFTER THE ACCIDENT AND BEFORE PROCEEDINGS

4.1 The claimant must take reasonable steps to establish whether there is in fact any insurance covering the use of the vehicle which caused the injury or damage. First, a claimant has statutory rights under section 154 of the Road Traffic Act 1988 to obtain relevant particulars which he must take steps to exercise even if that involves incurring expense and MIB will insist that he does so. See clause 13(a).

MIB accept that if the MIB application form is sufficiently completed and signed by the Claimant, the Claimant will have complied with this Clause of the Agreement.

4.2. Other steps will include the following:

4.2.1 The exchange of names, addresses and insurance particulars between those involved either at the scene of the accident or afterwards.

4.2.2 Corresponding with the owner or driver of the vehicle or his representatives. He will be obliged under the terms of his motor policy to inform his insurers and a letter of claim addressed to him will commonly be passed to the insurers who may reply on his behalf. See clause 9(2)(d).

4.2.3 Where only the vehicle's number is known, enquiry of the Driver and Vehicle Licensing Agency at Swansea SA99 1BP as to the registered keeper of the vehicle is desirable so that through him the identity of the owner or driver can be established or confirmed.

4.2.4 Enquiries of the police (see clause 13(b) *and Note 4.1 above*).

4.3 If enquiries show that there is an insurer who is obliged to accept and does accept the obligation to handle the claim against the user of the vehicle concerned, even though the relevant liability may not be covered by the policy in question, then the claim should be pursued with such insurer.

4.4 If, however, enquiries disclose that there is no insurance covering the use of the vehicle concerned or if the insurer cannot be identified or the insurer asserts that it is under no obligation to handle the claim or if for any other reason it is clear that the insurer will not satisfy any judgment, the claim should be directed to MIB itself.

5. WHEN PROCEEDINGS ARE COMMENCED OR CONTEMPLATED

5.1 As explained above, MIB does not have to wait for a judgment to be obtained before intervening. Claimants may apply to MIB before the commencement of proceedings. MIB will respond to any claim which complies with clause 7 and must give a reasoned reply to any request for compensation in respect of the claim (see clause 18) although normally a request for compensation will not be met until MIB is satisfied that it is properly based. Interim compensation payments are dealt with at paragraph 8 below.

Application Forms are available from MIB's office or their website: **www.mib.org.uk**.

Where a claim is made by the Claimant in person, who has not received legal advice, then if the claim is first made within 14 days prior to expiry of the limitation period, MIB will require the completed application form within the 21 days after the issue of proceedings.

5.2   It is important that wherever possible claims should be made using MIB's application form, fully completed and accompanied by documents supporting the claim, as soon as possible to avoid unnecessary delays. See clause 7(1). Copies of the form can be obtained on request made by post, telephone, fax or the DX or on personal application to MIB's offices.

5.3   The claimant must give MIB notice *in writing* that he has commenced legal proceedings. The notice, the completed application form (if appropriate) and all necessary documents must be received by MIB no later than 14 days after the date of commencement of proceedings. See clause 9(1) and (2)(a). The date of commencement is determined in accordance with the definitions of 'relevant proceedings' and 'commencement' given in clause 1.

When it is decided to commence legal proceedings, MIB should be joined as a defendent [sic] (unless there is good reason not to do so). Once MIB is a defendant, the Court will advise the relevant events direct and clauses 9(3), 11 and 12 will no longer apply.

The form of words set out below should be used for the joinder of MIB as second defendant:

1.   The Second Defendant is a Company limited by guarantee under the Companies Act. Pursuant to an Agreement with the Secretary of State for the Environment Transport and the Regions dated 13th August 1999, the Second Defendant provides compensation in certain circumstances to persons suffering injury or damage as a result of the negligence of uninsured motorists.
2.   The Claimant has used all reasonable endeavours to ascertain the liability of an insurer for the First Defendant and at the time of the commencement of these proceedings verily believes the First Defendant is not insured.
3.   The Claimant accepts that only if a final judgment is obtained against the First Defendant (which judgment is not satisfied in full within seven days from the date upon which the Claimant became entitled to enforce it) can the Second Defendant be required to satisfy the judgement and then only if the terms and conditions set out in the Agreement are satisfied. Until that time, any liability of the Second Defendant is only contingent.
4.   To avoid the Second Defendant having later to apply to join itself to this action (which the Claimant must consent to in any event, pursuant to Clause 14(b) of the Agreement) the Claimant seeks to include the Second Defendant from the outset recognising fully the Second Defendant's position as reflected in 3 above and the rights of the Second Defendant fully to participate in the action to protect its position as a separate party to the action.
5.   With the above in mind, the Claimant seeks a declaration of the Second Defendant's contingent liability to satisfy the claimant's judgment against the First Defendant.

5.4   This notice *must* have with it the following:

5.4.1 a copy of the document originating the proceedings, usually in England and Wales a Claim Form and in Scotland a Sheriff Court Writ or Court of Session Summons (see clause 9(2)(b));

5.4.2 normally the Particulars of Claim endorsed on or served with the Claim Form or Writ (see clause 9(2)(e), although this document may be served later in accordance with clause 9(3) if that applies);

5.4.3 in any case the documents required by the relevant rules of procedure (see clause 9(2)(f)).

Provided that the documents referred to above are forwarded to MIB, it is not necessary to enclose the Response Pack or the Notice of Issue.

5.5 In addition, other items as mentioned in clause 9(2), e. g. correspondence with the Defendant (or Defender) or his representatives, need to be supplied where appropriate.

5.6 It is for the claimant to satisfy himself that the notice has in fact been received by MIB. However, where the Claimant proves that service by DX, First Class Post, Personal Service or any other form of service allowed by the Civil Procedure Rules, was effected, MIB will accept that such notice has been served in the same circumstances in which a party to litigation would be obliged to accept that he had been validly served by such means.

5.7 It should be noted that when MIB has been given notice of a claim, it may elect to require the claimant to bring proceedings and attempt to secure a judgment against the party whom MIB alleges to be wholly or partly responsible for the loss or damage or who may be contracted to indemnify the claimant. In such a case MIB must indemnify the claimant against the costs of such proceedings. Subject to that, however, MIB's obligation to satisfy the judgment in the action will only arise if the claimant commences the proceedings and takes all reasonable steps to obtain a judgment. See clause 14(a).

6. SERVICE OF PROCEEDINGS

6.1 If proceedings are commenced in England or Wales the claimant must inform MIB of the date of service (see clause 10(1) and (2)).

6.2 If service of the Claim Form is effected by the Court, notice should be given within 7 days from the earliest of the dates listed in clause 10(3)(a)(i) or (ii) or within 14 days from the date mentioned in clause 10(3)(b) (the date of deemed service under the court's rules of procedure). Claimants are advised to take steps to ensure that the court or the defendant's legal representatives inform them of the date of service as soon as possible. Although a longer period is allowed than in other cases, service may be deemed to have occurred without a Claimant knowing of it until some time afterwards.

6.3 Where proceedings are served personally, notice should be given 7 days from the date of personal service (see clause 10(3)(a)(iii)).

6.4 However, by concession MIB will accept the notice referred to in note 6.1 above if it is received by MIB within 14 days from the dates referred to in notes 6.2 and 6.3.

6.5 In Scotland, proceedings are commenced at the date of service (see clause 1) so notice should already have been given under clause 9 and clause 10 does not apply there.

7. AFTER SERVICE AND BEFORE JUDGMENT

See Note 5.3 above.

7.1   Notice of the filing of a defence, of an amendment to the Statement or Particulars of Claim, and the setting down of the case for trial must be given not later than 7 days after the occurrence of such events and a copy of the document must be supplied (see clause 11(1)).

7.2   However, by concession MIB will accept the notice referred to in note 7.1 above if it is received by MIB within 14 days after the proven date on which it was received by the claimant.

7.3   MIB may request further information and documents to support the claim where it is not satisfied that the documents supplied with the application form are sufficient to enable it to assess its liability under the Agreement (see clause 11(2)).

7.4   If the claimant intends to sign or apply for judgment he must give MIB notice of the fact before doing so. This notice must be given at least 35 days before the application is to be made or the date when judgment is to be signed (see clause 12).
   The 35 days notice does not apply where the court enters judgment of its own motion.

7.5   At no time must the claimant oppose MIB if it wishes to be joined as a party to proceedings and he must if requested consent to any application by MIB to be joined. Conflicts may arise between a Defendant and MIB which require MIB to become a Defendant or, in Scotland, a party Minuter if a defence is be filed on its behalf (see clause 14(b)).

8.   INTERIM PAYMENTS

In substantial cases, the claimant may wish to apply for an interim payment. MIB will consider such applications on a voluntary basis but otherwise the claimant has the right to apply to the court for an interim payment order which, if granted, will be met by MIB.

9.   AFTER JUDGMENT

9.1   MIB's basic obligation normally arises if a judgment is not satisfied within 7 days after the claimant has become entitled to enforce it (see clause 1). However, that judgement may in certain circumstances be set aside and with it MIB's obligation to satisfy it. Sometimes MIB wishes to apply to set aside a judgment either wholly or partially. If MIB decides not to satisfy a judgment it will notify the claimant as soon as possible. Where a judgment is subsequently set aside, MIB will require the claimant to repay any sum previously paid by MIB to discharge its obligation under the Agreement (see clause 15(b)).

9.2   MIB is not obliged to satisfy a judgment unless the claimant has in return assigned the benefit to MIB or its nominee (see clause 15(a)). If such assignment is effected and if the subject matter of the judgment includes claims in respect of which MIB is not obliged to meet any judgment and if MIB effects any recovery on the judgment, the sum recovered will be divided between MIB and the claimant in proportion to the liabilities which were and which were not covered by MIB's obligation (see clause 21).

10.   PERMISSIBLE DEDUCTIONS FROM PAYMENTS BY MIB

10.1   Claims for loss and damage for which the claimant has been compensated or indemnified, e.g. under a contract of insurance or under the Policyholders Protection Act 1975, and which has not been taken into account in the judgment, may be deducted from the sum paid in settlement of MIB's obligation (see clause 17).

10.2   If there is a likelihood that the claimant will receive payment from such a source after the judgment has been satisfied by MIB, MIB will require him to undertake to repay any sum which duplicates the compensation assessed by the court (see clause 15(b)).

11.   UNTRACED DRIVERS

11.1   Where the owner or driver of a vehicle cannot be identified application may be made to MIB under the relevant Untraced Drivers Agreement. This provides, subject to specified conditions, for the payment of compensation for personal **injury**. It *does not* provide for compensation in respect of damage to property.

11.2   In those cases where it is unclear whether the owner or driver of a vehicle has been correctly identified it is sensible for the claimant to register a claim under both this Agreement and the Untraced Drivers Agreement following which MIB will advise which Agreement will, in its view, apply in the circumstances of the particular case.

The 2003 Untraced Drivers' Agreement

MOTOR INSURERS' BUREAU (COMPENSATION OF VICTIMS OF UNTRACED DRIVERS)

Text of an Agreement dated the 7th February 2003 between the Secretary of State for Transport and Motor Insurers' Bureau together with some notes on its scope and purpose

THIS AGREEMENT is made the seventh day of February 2003 between the SECRETARY OF STATE FOR TRANSPORT (hereinafter referred to as 'the Secretary of State') and the MOTOR INSURERS' BUREAU, whose registered office is at Linford Wood House 6–12 Capital Drive Linford Wood Milton Keynes MK14 6XT (hereinafter referred to as 'MIB').

IT IS HEREBY AGREED AS FOLLOWS:

INTERPRETATION

General interpretation

1.   (1)   In this Agreement, unless the context otherwise requires, the following expressions have the following meanings –

'1988 Act' means the Road Traffic Act 1988;

'1996 Agreement' means the Agreement made on 14 June 1996 between the Secretary of State for Transport and MIB providing for the compensation of victims of untraced drivers;

'1999 Agreement' means the Agreement dated 13th August 1999 made between the Secretary of State for the Environment, Transport and the Regions and MIB providing for the compensation of victims of uninsured drivers;

'applicant' means the person who has applied for compensation in respect of a death, bodily injury or damage to property (or the person on whose behalf such an application has been made) and 'application' means an application made by or on behalf of an applicant;

'arbitrator', where the arbitration takes place under Scottish law, includes an arbiter;

'award' means the aggregate of the sums which MIB is obliged to pay under this Agreement;

'bank holiday' means a day which is, or is to be observed as, a bank holiday under the Banking and Financial Dealings Act 1971;

'judgement' means, in relation to a court in Scotland, a court decree; 'property' means any property whether (in England and Wales) real or personal, or (in Scotland) heritable or moveable;

'relevant proceedings' means civil proceedings brought by the applicant (whether or not pursuant to a requirement made under this Agreement) against a person other than the unidentified person in respect of an event described in clause 4(1);

'specified excess' means £300 or such other sum as may from time to time be agreed in writing between the Secretary of State and MIB;

'unidentified person' means a person who is, or appears to be, wholly or partly liable in respect of the death, injury or damage to property to which an application relates and who cannot be identified.

(2) Save as otherwise herein provided, the Interpretation Act 1978 shall apply for the interpretation of this Agreement as it applies for the interpretation of an Act of Parliament.

(3) Where, under this Agreement, something is required to be done within a specified period after a date or the happening of a particular event, the period begins on the day after the happening of that event.

(4) Where, apart from this paragraph, the period in question, being a period of 7 days or less, would include a Saturday, Sunday, bank holiday, Christmas Day or Good Friday, that day shall be excluded.

(5) Save where expressly otherwise provided, a reference in this Agreement to a numbered clause is a reference to the clause bearing that number in this Agreement and a reference to a numbered paragraph is a reference to a paragraph bearing that number in the clause or schedule in which the reference occurs.

(6) In this Agreement –

(a) a reference (however framed) to the doing of any act or thing by or the happening of any event in relation to the applicant includes a reference to the doing of that act or thing by or the happening of that event in relation to a Solicitor or other person acting on his behalf, and

(b) a requirement to give notice or send documents to MIB shall, where MIB has appointed a Solicitor to act on its behalf in relation to the application, be satisfied by the giving of the notice or the sending of the documents, in the manner herein provided for, to that Solicitor.

Applicants' representatives

2. Where, under and in accordance with this Agreement –

(a) any notice or other document is given to or by a Solicitor or other person acting on behalf of an applicant,

(b) any act or thing is done by or in respect of such Solicitor or other person,

(c) any decision is made by or in respect of such Solicitor or other person, or

(d) any payment is made to such Solicitor or other person,

then, whatever may be the age or other circumstances affecting the capacity of the applicant, that act, thing, decision or payment shall be treated as if it had been done to or by, or made to or in respect of an applicant of full age and capacity.

APPLICATION OF AGREEMENT

Duration of Agreement

3. (1) This Agreement shall come into force on 14 February 2003.

97

(2) This Agreement may be determined by the Secretary of State or by MIB giving to the other not less than twelve months' notice in writing to that effect.

(3) Notwithstanding the giving of notice of determination under paragraph (2) this Agreement shall continue to operate in respect of any application made in respect of death, bodily injury or damage to property arising from an event occurring on or before the date of termination specified in the notice.

Scope of Agreement

4. (1) Save as provided in clause 5, this Agreement applies where –

    (a) the death of, or bodily injury to, a person or damage to any property of a person has been caused by, or arisen out of, the use of a motor vehicle on a road or other public place in Great Britain, and

    (b) the event giving rise to the death, bodily injury or damage to property occurred on or after 14 February 2003, and

    (c) the death, bodily injury or damage to property occurred in circumstances giving rise to liability of a kind which is required to be covered by a policy of insurance or a security under Part VI of the 1988 Act, and

    (d) it is not possible for the applicant –

        (i) to identify the person who is, or appears to be, liable in respect of the death, injury or damage, or

        (ii) (where more than one person is or appears to be liable) to identify any one or more of those persons,

    and

    (e) the applicant has made an application in writing to MIB for the payment of an award in respect of such death, bodily injury or damage to property (and in a case where they are applicable the requirements of paragraph (2) are satisfied), and

    (f) the conditions specified in paragraph (3), or such of those conditions as are relevant to the application, are satisfied.

(2) Where an application is signed by a person who is neither the applicant nor a Solicitor acting on behalf of the applicant MIB may refuse to accept the application (and shall incur no liability under this Agreement) until it is reasonably satisfied that, having regard to the status of the signatory and his relationship with the applicant, the applicant is fully aware of the content and effect of the application but subject thereto MIB shall not refuse to accept an application by reason only of the fact that it is signed by a person other than the applicant or his Solicitor.

(3) The conditions referred to in paragraph (1)(f) are that –

    (a) except in a case to which sub-paragraph (b) applies, the application must have been made not later than –

        (i) three years after the date of the event which is the subject of the application in the case of a claim for compensation for death or bodily injury (whether or not damage to property has also arisen from the same event), or

        (ii) nine months after the date of that event in the case of a claim for compensation for damage to property (whether or not death or bodily injury has also arisen from the same event);

    (b) in a case where the applicant could not reasonably have been expected to have become aware of the existence of bodily injury or damage to property, the application must have been made as soon as practicable after he did become (or ought reasonably to have become) aware of it and in any case not later than –

    (i)   fifteen years after the date of the event which is the subject of the application in the case of a claim for compensation for death or bodily injury (whether or not damage to property has also arisen from the same event), or

    (ii)   two years after the date of that event in the case of a claim for compensation for damage to property (whether or not death or bodily injury has also arisen from the same event);

(c)   the applicant, or a person acting on the applicant's behalf, must have reported that event to the police –

    (i)   in the case of an event from which there has arisen a death or bodily injury alone, not later than 14 days after its occurrence, and

    (ii)   in the case of an event from which there has arisen property damage (whether or not a death or bodily injury has also arisen from it), not later than 5 days after its occurrence,

but where that is not reasonably possible the event must have been reported as soon as reasonably possible;

(d)   the applicant must produce satisfactory evidence of having made the report required under sub-paragraph (c) in the form of an acknowledgement from the relevant force showing the crime or incident number under which that force has recorded the matter;

(e)   after making, or authorising the making of, a report to the police the applicant must have co-operated with the police in any investigation they have made into the event.

(4)   Where both death or bodily injury and damage to property have arisen from a single event nothing contained in this clause shall require an applicant to make an application in respect of the death or bodily injury on the same occasion as an application in respect of the damage to property and where two applications are made in respect of one event the provisions of this Agreement shall apply separately to each of them.

Exclusions from Agreement

5.   (1)   This Agreement does not apply where an application is made in any of the following circumstances (so that where an application is made partly in such circumstances and partly in other circumstances, it applies only to the part made in those other circumstances) –

(a)   where the applicant makes no claim for compensation in respect of death or bodily injury and the damage to property in respect of which compensation is claimed has been caused by, or has arisen out of, the use of an unidentified vehicle;

(b)   where the death, bodily injury or damage to property in respect of which the application is made has been caused by or has arisen out of the use of a motor vehicle which at the time of the event giving rise to such death, injury or damage was owned by or in the possession of the Crown, unless at that time some other person had undertaken responsibility for bringing into existence a policy of insurance or security satisfying the requirements of the 1988 Act;

(c)   where, at the time of the event in respect of which the application is made the person suffering death, injury or damage to property was voluntarily allowing himself to be carried in the responsible vehicle and before the commencement of his journey in the vehicle (or after such commencement if he could reasonably be expected to have alighted from the vehicle) he knew or ought to have known that the vehicle –

       (i)   had been stolen or unlawfully taken, or

       (ii)   was being used without there being in force in relation to its use a contract of insurance or security which complied with the 1988 Act, or

       (iii)   was being used in the course or furtherance of crime, or

       (iv)   was being used as a means of escape from or avoidance of lawful apprehension;

(d)   where the death, bodily injury or damage to property was caused by, or in the course of, an act of terrorism;

(e)   where property damaged as a result of the event giving rise to the application is insured against such damage and the applicant has recovered the full amount of his loss from the insurer on or before the date of the application (but without prejudice to the application of the Agreement in the case of any other claim for compensation made in respect of the same event);

(f)   where a claim is made for compensation in respect of damage to a motor vehicle (or losses arising therefrom) and, at the time when the damage to it was sustained –

       (i)   there was not in force in relation to the use of that vehicle such a contract of insurance as is required by Part VI of the 1988 Act, and

       (ii)   the person suffering damage to property either knew or ought to have known that was the case

    (but without prejudice to the application of the Agreement in the case of any other claim for compensation made in respect of the same event);

(g)   where the application is made neither by a person suffering injury or property damage nor by the personal representative of such a person nor by a dependant claiming in respect of the death of another person but is made in any of the following circumstances, namely –

       (i)   where a cause of action or a judgment has been assigned to the applicant, or

       (ii)   where the applicant is acting pursuant to a right of subrogation or a similar contractual or other right belonging to him.

(2)   The burden of proving that the person suffering death, injury or damage to property knew or ought to have known of any matter set out in paragraph (1)(c) shall be on MIB but, in the absence of evidence to the contrary, proof by MIB of any of the following matters shall be taken as proof of his knowledge of the matter set out in paragraph (1)(c)(ii) –

    (a)   that he was the owner or registered keeper of the vehicle or had caused or permitted its use;

    (b)   that he knew the vehicle was being used by a person who was below the minimum age at which he could be granted a licence authorising the driving of a vehicle of that class;

    (c)   that he knew that the person driving the vehicle was disqualified for holding or obtaining a driving licence;

(d)   that he knew that the user of the vehicle was neither its owner nor registered keeper nor an employee of the owner or registered keeper nor the owner or registered keeper of any other vehicle.

(3) Where –

(a)   the application includes a claim for compensation both in respect of death or bodily injury and also in respect of damage to property, and

(b)   the death or injury and the property damage has been caused by, or has arisen out of, the use of an unidentified vehicle,

the Agreement does not apply to the claim for compensation in respect of the damage to property.

(4) For the purposes of paragraphs (1) and (2) –

(a)   references to a person being carried in a vehicle include references to his being carried in or upon, or entering or getting on to or alighting from the vehicle;

(b)   knowledge which a person has or ought to have for the purposes of sub-paragraph (c) includes knowledge of matters which he could reasonably be expected to have been aware of had he not been under the self-induced influence of drink or drugs;

(c)   'crime' does not include the commission of an offence under the Traffic Acts, except an offence under section 143 (use of a motor vehicle on a road without there being in force a policy of insurance), and 'Traffic Acts' means the Road Traffic Regulation Act 1984, the Road Traffic Act 1988 and the Road Traffic Offenders Act 1988;

(d)   'responsible vehicle' means the vehicle the use of which caused (or through the use of which there arose) the death, bodily injury or damage to property which is the subject of the application;

(e)   'terrorism' has the meaning given in section 1 of the Terrorism Act 2000;

(f)   'dependant' has the same meaning as in section 1(3) of the Fatal Accidents Act 1976.

Limitation on application of Agreement

6. (1) This clause applies where an applicant receives compensation or other payment in respect of the death, bodily injury or damage to property otherwise than in the circumstances described in clause 5(1)(e) from any of the following persons –

(a)   an insurer or under an insurance policy (other than a life assurance policy) or arrangement between the applicant or his employer and the insurer, or

(b)   a person who has given a security pursuant to the requirements of the 1988 Act under an agreement between the applicant and the security giver, or

(c)   any other source other than a person who is an identified person for the purposes of clauses 13 to 15 or an insurer of, or a person who has given a security on behalf of, such a person.

(2) Where the compensation or other payment received is equal to or greater than the amount which MIB would otherwise be liable to pay under the provisions of clauses 8 and 9 MIB shall have no liability under those provisions (to the intent that this Agreement shall immediately cease to apply except to the extent that the applicant is entitled to a contribution to his legal costs under clause 10).

(3) Where the compensation or other payment received is less than the amount which MIB would otherwise be liable to pay under the provisions of clauses 8 and 9

MIB's liability under those provisions shall be reduced by an amount equal to that compensation or payment.

PRINCIPAL TERMS AND CONDITIONS

MIB's obligation to investigate claims and determine amount of award

7. (1) MIB shall, at its own cost, take all reasonable steps to investigate the claim made in the application and –

   (a) if it is satisfied after conducting a preliminary investigation that the case is not one to which this Agreement applies and the application should be rejected, it shall inform the applicant accordingly and (subject to the following provisions of this Agreement) need take no further action, or

   (b) in any other case, it shall conduct a full investigation and shall as soon as reasonably practicable having regard to the availability of evidence make a report on the applicant's claim.

   (2) Subject to the following paragraphs of this clause, MIB shall, on the basis of the report and, where applicable, any relevant proceedings –

   (a) reach a decision as to whether it must make an award to the applicant in respect of the death, bodily injury or damage to property, and

   (b) where it decides to make an award, determine the amount of that award.

   (3) Where MIB reaches a decision that the Agreement applies and that it is able to calculate the whole amount of the award the report shall be treated as a full report and the award shall (subject to the following provisions of this Agreement) be treated as a full and final award.

   (4) Where MIB reaches a decision that the Agreement applies and that it should make an award but further decides that it is not at that time able to calculate the final amount of the award (or a part thereof), it may designate the report as an interim report and where it does so –

   (a) it may, as soon as reasonably practicable, make one or more further interim reports, but

   (b) it must, as soon as reasonably practicable having regard to the availability of evidence, make a final report.

   (5) Where it makes an interim or final report MIB shall, on the basis of that report and, where applicable, any relevant proceedings –

   (a) in the case of an interim report, determine the amount of any interim award it wishes to make, and

   (b) in the case of its final report, determine the whole amount of its award which shall (subject to the following provisions of this Agreement) be treated as a full and final award.

   (6) MIB shall be under an obligation to make an award only if it is satisfied, on the balance of probabilities, that the death, bodily injury or damage to property was caused in such circumstances that the unidentified person would (had he been identified) have been held liable to pay damages to the applicant in respect of it.

   (7) MIB shall determine the amount of its award in accordance with the provisions of clauses 8 to 10 and (in an appropriate case) clauses 12 to 14 but shall not thereby be under a duty to calculate the exact proportion of the award which represents compensation, interest or legal costs.

Compensation

8.　(1)　MIB shall include in its award to the applicant, by way of compensation for the death, bodily injury or damage to property, a sum equivalent to the amount which a court –

　　　(a)　applying the law of England and Wales, in a case where the event giving rise to the death, injury or damage occurred in England or Wales, or

　　　(b)　applying the law of Scotland, in a case where that event occurred in Scotland,

　　would have awarded to the applicant (where applying English law) as general and special damages or (where applying the law of Scotland) as solatium and patrimonial loss if the applicant had brought successful proceedings to enforce a claim for damages against the unidentified person.

　　(2)　In calculating the sum payable under paragraph (1), MIB shall adopt the same method of calculation as the court would adopt in calculating damages but it shall be under no obligation to include in that calculation an amount in respect of loss of earnings suffered by the applicant to the extent that he has been paid wages or salary (or any sum in lieu of them) whether or not such payments were made subject to an agreement or undertaking on his part to repay the same in the event of his recovering damages for the loss of those earnings.

　　(3)　Where an application includes a claim in respect of damage to property, MIB's liability in respect of that claim shall be limited in accordance with the following rules –

　　　(a)　if the loss incurred by an applicant in respect of any one event giving rise to a claim does not exceed the specified excess, MIB shall incur no liability to that applicant in respect of that event;

　　　(b)　if the aggregate of all losses incurred by both the applicant and other persons in respect of any one event giving rise to a claim ('the total loss') exceeds the specified excess but does not exceed £250,000 –

　　　　　(i)　MIB's liability to an individual applicant shall be the amount of the claim less the specified excess, and

　　　　　(ii)　MIB's total liability to applicants in respect of claims arising from that event shall be the total loss less a sum equal to the specified excess multiplied by the number of applicants who have incurred loss through damage to property;

　　　(c)　if the total loss exceeds £250,000 –

　　　　　(i)　MIB's liability to an individual applicant shall not exceed the amount of the claim less the specified excess, and

　　　　　(ii)　MIB's total liability to applicants in respect of claims arising from that event shall be £250,000 less a sum equal to the specified excess multiplied by the number of applicants who have incurred loss due to property damage.

　　(4)　MIB shall not be liable to pay compensation to an appropriate authority in respect of any loss incurred by that authority as a result of its failure to recover a charge for the recovery, storage or disposal of an abandoned vehicle under a power contained in the Refuse Disposal (Amenity) Act 1978 or Part VIII of the Road Traffic Regulation Act 1984 (and in this paragraph 'appropriate authority' has the meaning given in the Act under which the power to recover the charge was exercisable).

Interest

9.   (1)   MIB shall in an appropriate case also include in the award a sum representing interest on the compensation payable under clause 8 at a rate equal to that which a court –

      (a)   applying the law of England and Wales, in a case where the event giving rise to the death, bodily injury or damage to property occurred in England or Wales, or

      (b)   applying the law of Scotland, in a case where that event occurred in Scotland,

would have awarded to a successful applicant.

    (2)   MIB is not required by virtue of paragraph (1) to pay a sum representing interest in respect of the period before the date which is one month after the date on which MIB receives the police report (but, where MIB has failed to seek and obtain that report promptly after the date of the application, interest shall run from the date which falls one month after the date on which it would have received it had it acted promptly).

Contribution towards legal costs

10.   (1)   MIB shall, in a case where it has decided to make a compensation payment under clause 8, also include in the award a sum by way of contribution towards the cost of obtaining legal advice from a Solicitor, Barrister or Advocate in respect of –

      (a)   the making of an application under this Agreement;

      (b)   the correctness of a decision made by MIB under this Agreement; or

      (c)   the adequacy of an award (or a part thereof) offered by MIB under this Agreement

that sum to be determined in accordance with the Schedule to this Agreement.

    (2)   MIB shall not be under a duty to make a payment under paragraph (1) unless it is satisfied that the applicant did obtain legal advice in respect of any one or more of the matters specified in that paragraph.

Conditions precedent to MIB's obligations

11.   (1)   The applicant must –

      (a)   make his application in such form,

      (b)   provide in support of the application such statements and other information (whether in writing or orally at interview), and

      (c)   give such further assistance,

as may reasonably be required by MIB or by any person acting on MIB's behalf to enable an investigation to be carried out under clause 7 of this Agreement.

    (2)   The applicant must provide MIB with written authority to take all such steps as may be reasonably necessary in order to carry out a proper investigation of the claim.

    (3)   The applicant must, if MIB reasonably requires him to do so before reaching a decision under clause 7, provide MIB with a statutory declaration, made by him, setting out to the best of his knowledge and belief all the facts and circumstances upon which his application is based or such facts and circumstances in relation to the application as MIB may reasonably specify.

(4) The applicant must, if MIB reasonably requires him to do so before it reaches a decision or determination under clause 7 and subject to the following provisions of this clause –

   (a) at MIB's option (and subject to paragraph (5)) either –

      (i) bring proceedings against any person or persons who may, in addition or alternatively to the unidentified person, be liable to the applicant in respect of the death, bodily injury or damage to property (by virtue of having caused or contributed to that death, injury or damage, by being vicariously liable in respect of it or having failed to effect third party liability insurance in respect of the vehicle in question) and co-operate with MIB in taking such steps as are reasonably necessary to obtain judgement in those proceedings, or

      (ii) authorise MIB to bring such proceedings and take such steps in the applicant's name;

   (b) at MIB's expense, provide MIB with a transcript of any official shorthand or recorded note taken in those proceedings of any evidence given or judgement delivered therein;

   (c) assign to MIB or to its nominee the benefit of any judgement obtained by him (whether or not obtained in proceedings brought under sub-paragraph (a) above) in respect of the death, bodily injury or damage to property upon such terms as will secure that MIB or its nominee will be accountable to the applicant for any amount by which the aggregate of all sums recovered by MIB or its nominee under the judgement (after deducting all reasonable expenses incurred in effecting recovery) exceeds the award made by MIB under this Agreement in respect of that death, injury or damage;

   (d) undertake to assign to MIB the right to any sum which is or may be due from an insurer, security giver or other person by way of compensation for, or benefit in respect of, the death, bodily injury or damage to property and which would (if payment had been made before the date of the award) have excluded or limited MIB's liability under the provisions of clause 6.

(5) If, pursuant to paragraph (4)(a), MIB requires the applicant to bring proceedings or take steps against any person or persons (or to authorise MIB to bring such proceedings or take such steps in his name) MIB shall indemnify the applicant against all costs and expenses reasonably incurred by him in complying with that requirement.

(6) Where the applicant, without having been required to do so by MIB, has commenced proceedings against any person described in paragraph (4)(a) –

   (a) the applicant shall as soon as reasonably possible notify MIB of such proceedings and provide MIB with such further information about them as MIB may reasonably require, and

   (b) the applicant's obligations in paragraph (4)(a) to (c) shall apply in respect of such proceedings as if they had been brought at MIB's request.

JOINT AND SEVERAL LIABILITY

Joint and several liability: interpretation

12. In clauses 13 to 15 –

'identified person' includes an identified employer or principal of a person who is himself unidentified;

'original judgement' means a judgement obtained against an identified person at first instance in relevant proceedings;

'three month period' means the period of three months specified in clause 13(3); and

'unidentified person's liability' means –

(a) the amount of the contribution which (if not otherwise apparent) would, on the balance of probabilities, have been recoverable from the unidentified person in an action brought –

    (i)   in England and Wales, under the Civil Liability (Contribution) Act 1978, or

    (ii)   in Scotland, under the Law Reform (Miscellaneous Provisions) (Scotland) Act 1940,

by an identified person who had been held liable in full in an earlier action brought by the applicant, and

(b) where a court has awarded the applicant interest or costs in addition to damages, an appropriate proportion of that interest or those costs.

MIB's liability where wrongdoer is identified

13. (1) This clause applies where the death, bodily injury or damage to property in respect of which the application is made is caused, or appears on the balance of probabilities to have been caused –

    (a)   partly by an unidentified person and partly by an identified person, or

    (b)   partly by an unidentified person and partly by another unidentified person whose employer or principal is identified,

in circumstances making (or appearing to make) the identified person liable, or vicariously liable, to the applicant in respect of the death, injury or damage.

(2) Where this clause applies, MIB's liability under this Agreement shall not exceed the unidentified person's liability and the following provisions shall apply to determine MIB's liability in specific cases.

(3) Where the applicant has obtained a judgement in relevant proceedings in respect of the death, injury or damage which has not been satisfied in full by or on behalf of the identified person within the period of three months after the date on which the applicant became entitled to enforce it –

    (a)   if that judgement is wholly unsatisfied within the three month period MIB shall make an award equal to the unidentified person's liability;

    (b)   if the judgement is satisfied in part only within the three month period, MIB shall make an award equal to –

        (i)   the unsatisfied part, if it does not exceed the unidentified person's liability; and

        (ii)   the unidentified person's liability, if the unsatisfied part exceeds the unidentified person's liability.

(4) A judgement given in any relevant proceedings against an identified person shall be conclusive as to any issue determined in those proceedings which is relevant to the determination of MIB's liability under this Agreement.

(5) Where the applicant has not obtained (or been required by MIB to obtain) a judgement in respect of the death, injury or damage against the identified person but has received an agreed payment from the identified person in respect of the death, bodily injury or damage to property, that payment shall be treated for the purposes of this Agreement as a full settlement of the applicant's claim and MIB shall be under no liability under this Agreement in respect thereof.

(6)   Where the applicant has not obtained (or been required by MIB to obtain) a judgement in respect of the death, injury or damage against the identified person nor received any payment by way of compensation in respect thereof from the identified person MIB shall make an award equal to the unidentified person's liability.

Appeals by identified persons

14.   (1)   This clause applies where an appeal against, or other proceeding to set aside, the original judgement is commenced within the three month period.

(2)   If, as a result of the appeal or other proceeding –

(a)   the applicant ceases to be entitled to receive any payment in respect of the death, bodily injury or damage to property from any identified person, clause 13 shall apply as if he had neither obtained nor been required by MIB to obtain a judgement against that person;

(b)   the applicant becomes entitled to recover an amount different from that which he was entitled to recover under the original judgement the provisions of clause 13(3) shall apply, but as if for each of the references therein to the original judgement there were substituted a reference to the judgement in that appeal or other proceeding;

(c)   the applicant remains entitled to enforce the original judgement the provisions of clause 13(3) shall apply, but as if for each of the references therein to the three month period there were substituted a reference to the period of three months after the date on which the appeal or other proceeding was disposed of.

(3)   Where the judgement in the appeal or other proceeding is itself the subject of a further appeal or similar proceeding the provisions of this clause shall apply in relation to that further appeal or proceeding in the same manner as they apply in relation to the first appeal or proceeding.

(4)   Nothing in this clause shall oblige MIB to make a payment to the applicant until the appeal or other proceeding has been determined.

Compensation recovered under Uninsured Drivers Agreements

15.   (1)   Where, in a case to which clause 13 applies, judgement in the relevant proceedings is given against an identified person in circumstances which render MIB liable to satisfy that judgement under any of the Uninsured Drivers Agreements, MIB shall not be under any liability under this Agreement in respect of the event to which the relevant proceedings relate.

(2)   In this clause 'Uninsured Drivers Agreements' means –

(a)   the Agreement dated 21st December 1988 made between the Secretary of State for Transport and MIB providing for the compensation of victims of uninsured drivers,

(b)   the 1999 Agreement, and

(c)   any agreement made between the Secretary of State and MIB (or their respective successors) which supersedes (whether immediately or otherwise) the 1999 Agreement.

NOTIFICATION OF DECISION AND PAYMENT OF AWARD

Notification of decision

16. MIB shall give the applicant notice of a decision or determination under clause 7 in writing and when so doing shall provide him –

  (a) if the application is rejected because a preliminary investigation has disclosed that it is not one made in a case to which this Agreement applies, with a statement to that effect;

  (b) if the application has been fully investigated, with a statement setting out –

  (i) all the evidence obtained during the investigation, and

  (ii) MIB's findings of fact from that evidence which are relevant to the decision;

  (c) if it has decided to make an interim award on the basis of an interim report under clause 7(4), with a copy of the report and a statement of the amount of the interim award;

  (d) if it has decided to make a full report under clause 7(3) or a final report under clause 7(4)(b), with a copy of the report and a statement of the amount of the full and final award;

  (e) in a case to which clause 13 applies, with a statement setting out the way in which the amount of the award has been computed under the provisions of that clause; and

  (f) in every case, with a statement of its reasons for making the decision or determination.

Acceptance of decision and payment of award

17. (1) Subject to the following paragraphs of this clause, if MIB gives notice to the applicant that it has decided to make an award to him, it shall pay him that award –

  (a) in the case of an interim award made pursuant to clause 7(5)(a), as soon as reasonably practicable after the making of the interim report to which the award relates;

  (b) in the case of a full and final award made pursuant to clause 7(3) or (5)(b) –

  (i) where the applicant notifies MIB in writing that he accepts the offer of the award unconditionally, not later than 14 days after the date on which MIB receives that acceptance, or

  (ii) where the applicant does not notify MIB of his acceptance in accordance with sub-paragraph (a) but the period during which he may give notice of an appeal under clause 19 has expired without such notice being given, not later than 14 days after the date of expiry of that period,

  and that payment shall discharge MIB from all liability under this Agreement in respect of the death, bodily injury or damage to property for which the award is made.

  (2) MIB may, upon notifying an applicant of its decision to make an award, offer to pay the award in instalments in accordance with a structure described in the decision letter (the 'structured settlement') and if the applicant notifies MIB in writing of his acceptance of the offer –

(a) the first instalment of the payment under the structured settlement shall be made not later than 14 days after the date on which MIB receives that acceptance, and

(b) subsequent payments shall be made in accordance with the agreed structure.

(3) Where an applicant has suffered bodily injury and believes either that there is a risk that he will develop a disease or condition other than that in respect of which he has made a claim or that a disease or condition in respect of which he has made a claim will deteriorate, he may –

(a) by notice given in his application, or

(b) by notice in writing received by MIB before the date on which MIB issues notification of its full or (as the case may be) final report under clause 16,

state that he wishes MIB to make a provisional award and if he does so paragraphs (4) and (5) shall apply.

(4) The applicant must specify in the notice given under paragraph (3) –

(a) each disease and each type of deterioration which he believes may occur, and

(b) the period during or within which he believes it may occur.

(5) Where MIB receives a notice under paragraph (3) it shall, not later than 14 days after the date of such receipt (or within such longer period as the applicant may agree) –

(a) accept the notice and confirm that any award it makes (other than an interim award made pursuant to clause 7(5)(a)) is to be treated as a provisional award, or

(b) reject the notice and inform the applicant that it is not willing to make a provisional award.

(6) Where MIB has notified the applicant that it accepts the notice, an award which would otherwise be treated as a full or final award under this Agreement shall be treated as a provisional award only and the applicant may make a supplementary application under this Agreement but –

(a) only in respect of a disease or a type of deterioration of his condition specified in his notice, and

(b) not later than the expiration of the period specified in his notice.

(7) Where MIB has notified the applicant that it rejects the notice, subject to any decision to the contrary made by an arbitrator, no award which MIB makes shall be treated as a provisional award.

APPEALS AGAINST MIB'S DECISION

Right of appeal

18. Where an applicant is not willing to accept –

(a) a decision or determination made by MIB under clause 7 or a part thereof, or

(b) a proposal for a structured settlement or a rejection of the applicant's request for a provisional award under clause 17,

he may give notice (a 'notice of appeal') that he wishes to submit the matter to arbitration in accordance with the provisions of clauses 19 to 25.

Notice of appeal

19. (1) A notice of appeal shall be given in writing to MIB at any time before the expiration of a period of 6 weeks from –

    (a) the date on which the applicant receives notice of MIB's decision under clause 16;
    (b) where he disputes a notification given under clause 17(5)(b), the date when such notification is given;
    (c) in any other case, the date on which he is given notification of the decision, determination or requirement.

    (2) The notice of appeal –

    (a) shall state the grounds on which the appeal is made,
    (b) shall contain the applicant's observations on MIB's decision,
    (c) may be accompanied by such further evidence in support of the appeal as the applicant thinks fit, and
    (d) shall contain an undertaking that (subject, in the case of an arbitration to be conducted in England and Wales, to his rights under sections 67 and 68 of the Arbitration Act 1996) the applicant will abide by the decision of the arbitrator made under this Agreement.

Procedure following notice of appeal

20. (1) Not later than 7 days after receiving the notice of appeal MIB shall –

    (a) apply to the Secretary of State for the appointment of a single arbitrator, or
    (b) having notified the applicant of its intention to do so, cause an investigation to be made into any further evidence supplied by the applicant and report to the applicant upon that investigation and of any change in its decision which may result from it.

    (2) Where the only ground stated in the notice of appeal is that the award is insufficient (including a ground contesting the degree of contributory negligence attributed to the applicant or, as the case may be, the person in respect of whose death the application is made), MIB may give notice to the applicant of its intention, if the appeal proceeds to arbitration, to ask the arbitrator to decide whether its award exceeds what a court would have awarded or whether the case is one in which it would make an award at all and shall in that notice set out such observations on that matter as MIB considers relevant to the arbitrator's decision.

    (3) Where MIB has made a report under paragraph (1)(b) or given to the applicant notice under paragraph (2), the applicant may, not later than 6 weeks after the date on which the report or (as the case may be) the notice was given to him –

    (a) notify MIB that he wishes to withdraw the appeal, or
    (b) notify MIB that he wishes to continue with the appeal and send with that notification –

        (i) any observations on the report made under paragraph (1)(b) which he wishes to have drawn to the attention of the arbitrator,
        (ii) any observations on the contents of the notice given under paragraph (2), including any further evidence not previously made available to MIB and relevant to the matter, which he wishes to have drawn to the attention of the arbitrator.

    (4) Where the applicant notifies MIB under paragraph (3)(b) of his wish to continue

the appeal, or if the applicant fails within the specified period of 6 weeks to give notification of his wish either to withdraw or to continue with the appeal, MIB shall, not later than 7 days after receiving the notification or 7 days after the expiry of the said period (as the case may be) –

(a)   apply to the Secretary of State for the appointment of an arbitrator, or

(b)   having notified the applicant of its intention to do so, cause a further investigation to be made into the further evidence sent under paragraph (3)(b)(ii).

(5)   Where MIB has caused an investigation to be made into any further evidence supplied by the applicant under paragraph (3)(b)(ii), it shall report to the applicant upon that investigation and of any change in a decision or determination made under clause 7 which may result from it and the applicant may, not later than 6 weeks after the date on which he receives the report –

(a)   notify MIB that he wishes to withdraw the appeal, or

(b)   notify MIB that he wishes to continue with the appeal.

(6)   Where the applicant notifies MIB under paragraph (5)(b) of his wish to continue the appeal, or if the applicant fails within the specified period of 6 weeks to give notification of his wish either to withdraw or to continue with the appeal, MIB shall not later than 7 days after receiving the notification or 7 days after the expiry of the said period (as the case may be) apply to the Secretary of State for the appointment of an arbitrator.

(7)   When applying to the Secretary of State for the appointment of an arbitrator MIB may send with the application such written observations as it wishes to make upon the applicant's notice of appeal but must at the same time send a copy of those observations to the applicant.

Appointment of arbitrator

21.   (1)   In the event of MIB neither applying to the Secretary of State for the appointment of an arbitrator in accordance with the provisions of clause 20 nor taking such further steps as it may at its discretion take in accordance with that clause, the applicant may apply to the Secretary of State for the appointment of an arbitrator.

(2)   For the purposes of the Arbitration Act 1996 (where the arbitration is to be conducted in England and Wales) the arbitral proceedings are to be regarded as commencing on the date of the making of the application by the Secretary of State or the applicant (as the case may be).

(3)   The Secretary of State shall, upon the making of an application for the appointment of an arbitrator to hear the appeal, appoint the first available member, by rotation, of a panel of Queen's Counsel appointed for the purpose of determining appeals under this Agreement (where the event giving rise to the death, bodily injury or damage to property occurred in England and Wales) by the Lord Chancellor or (where the event giving rise to the death, bodily injury or damage to property occurred in Scotland) by the Lord Advocate and shall forthwith notify the applicant and MIB of the appointment.

Arbitration procedure

22.   (1)   Upon receiving notification from the Secretary of State of the appointment of an arbitrator, MIB shall send to the arbitrator –

(a)   the notice of appeal,

(b)   (if appropriate) its request for a decision as to whether its award exceeds what a court would have awarded or whether the case is one in which it would make an award at all,

(c)   copies of –

    (i)   the applicant's application,

    (ii)   its decision, and

    (iii)   all statements, declarations, notices, reports, observations and transcripts of evidence made or given under this Agreement by the applicant or MIB.

(2)   The arbitrator may, if it appears to him to be necessary or expedient for the purpose of resolving any issue, ask MIB to make a further investigation and to submit a written report of its findings to him for his consideration and in such a case –

(a)   MIB shall undertake the investigation and send copies of the report to the arbitrator and the applicant,

(b)   the applicant may, not later than 4 weeks after the date on which a copy of the report is received by him, submit written observations on it to the arbitrator and if he does so he shall send a copy of those observations to MIB.

(3)   The arbitrator shall, after considering the written submissions referred to in paragraphs (1) and (2), send to the applicant and MIB a preliminary decision letter setting out the decision he proposes to make under clause 23 and his reasons for doing so.

(4)   Not later than 28 days after the date of sending of the preliminary decision letter (or such later date as the applicant and MIB may agree) the applicant and MIB may, by written notification given to the arbitrator and copied to the other, either –

(a)   accept the preliminary decision, or

(b)   submit written observations upon the preliminary decision or the reasons or both, or

(c)   request an oral hearing,

and if either of them should within that period fail to do any of those things (including a failure to provide the other person with a copy of his notification) he or it shall be treated as having accepted the decision.

(5)   If the applicant submits new evidence with any written observations under paragraph (4)(b) MIB may at its discretion, but within 28 days or such longer period as the arbitrator may allow, do any of the following –

(a)   make an investigation into that evidence,

(b)   submit its own written observations on that evidence, and

(c)   if it has not already done so, request an oral hearing,

and, except where an oral hearing has been requested, the arbitrator shall (in exercise of his powers under section 34 of the Arbitration Act 1996 if the arbitration is being conducted in England and Wales) determine whether, and if so how, such evidence shall be admitted and tested.

(6)   If both the applicant and MIB accept the reasoned preliminary decision that decision shall be treated as his final decision for the purposes of clause 23 (so that clause 23(2) shall not then apply) but if either of them submits observations on that decision the arbitrator must take those observations into account before making a final decision.

(7)   If the applicant or MIB requests an oral hearing, the arbitrator shall determine the appeal in that manner and in such a case –

(a)   the hearing shall be held in public unless the applicant requests that it (or any part of it) be heard in private;

(b)   the hearing shall take place at a location –

    (i)   in England or Wales, where the event giving rise to the death, bodily injury or damage to property occurred in England or Wales and the applicant is resident in England or Wales,

    (ii)   in Scotland, where the event giving rise to the death, bodily injury or damage to property occurred in Scotland and the applicant is resident in Scotland, or

    (iii)   in England, Wales or Scotland in any other case,

    which in the opinion of the arbitrator (after consultation with each of them) is convenient for both MIB and the applicant as well as for himself;

(c)   a party to the hearing may be represented by a lawyer or other person of that party's choosing;

(d)   a party to the hearing shall be entitled to address the arbitrator, to call witnesses and to put questions to those witnesses and any other person called as a witness.

Arbitrator's decision

23. (1) The arbitrator, having regard to the subject matter of the proceedings, may in an appropriate case –

    (a)   determine whether or not the case is one to which this Agreement applies;

    (b)   remit the application to MIB for a full investigation and a decision in accordance with the provisions of this Agreement;

    (c)   determine whether MIB should make an award under this Agreement and if so what that award should be;

    (d)   determine such other questions as have been referred to him as he thinks fit,

    (e)   (subject to the provisions of paragraph (4) of this clause and clause 24) order that the costs of the proceedings shall be paid by one party or allocated between the parties in such proportions as he thinks fit;

    and where the arbitrator makes a determination under sub-paragraph (a) that the case is one to which this Agreement applies, all the provisions of this Agreement shall apply as if the case were one to which clause 7(1)(b) applies.

  (2) The arbitrator shall notify MIB and the applicant of his decision in writing.

  (3) MIB shall pay to the applicant any amount which the arbitrator has decided shall be awarded to him, and that payment shall discharge MIB from all liability under this Agreement in respect of the death, bodily injury or damage to property in respect of which that decision is given.

  (4) Where an oral hearing has taken place at the request of the applicant and the arbitrator is satisfied that it was unnecessary and that the matter could have been decided on the basis of the written submissions referred to in clause 22(1) and (2) he shall take that into account when making an order under paragraph (1)(e).

Payment of arbitrator's fee and costs of legal representation

24. (1) Subject to paragraph (2), MIB shall upon being notified of the decision of the arbitrator pay the arbitrator a fee approved by the Lord Chancellor or the Lord Advocate, as the case may be, after consultation with MIB.

  (2) In a case where it appears to the arbitrator that, having regard to all the surrounding

circumstances of the case, there were no reasonable grounds for making the appeal or bringing the question before him, the arbitrator may, in his discretion, order –

(a) the applicant or,

(b) where he considers it appropriate to do so, any Solicitor or other person acting on behalf of the applicant,

to reimburse MIB the fee it has paid to the arbitrator or any part thereof.

(3) Where, pursuant to paragraph (2), the arbitrator orders –

(a) the applicant to reimburse MIB, MIB may deduct an amount equal to the fee from any amount which it pays to the applicant to discharge its liability under this Agreement;

(b) a Solicitor or other person to reimburse MIB, MIB may deduct an amount equal to the fee from any amount which it pays to that Soicitor or other person to discharge its liability to the applicant under this Agreement.

(4) Where there is an oral hearing and the applicant secures an award of compensation greater than that previously offered, then (unless the arbitrator orders otherwise) MIB shall make a contribution of £500 per half day towards the cost incurred by the applicant in respect of representation by a Solicitor, Barrister or Advocate.

Applicants under a disability

25. (1) If in any case it appears to MIB that, by reason of the applicant being a minor or of any other circumstance affecting his capacity to manage his affairs, it would be in the applicant's interest that all or some part of the award should be administered for him by an appropriate representative, MIB may establish for that purpose a trust of the whole or part of the award (such trust to take effect for such period and under such provisions as appears to MIB to be appropriate in the circumstances of the case) or, as the case may be, initiate or cause any other person to initiate the proceedings necessary to have the award administered by an appropriate representative and otherwise cause any amount payable under the award to be paid to and administered by the appropriate representative.

(2) In this clause 'appropriate representative' means –

(a) in England and Wales –

(i) the Family Welfare Association, or a similar body or person, as trustee of the trust, or

(ii) the Court of Protection; and

(b) in Scotland –

(i) a Judicial Factor, or

(ii) a guardian under the Adults with Incapacity (Scotland) Act 2000, or

(iii) (where the applicant is a child) the tutor or curator of the child or a person having parental responsibilities under the Children (Scotland) Act 1995.

ACCELERATED PROCEDURE

Instigation of accelerated procedure

26. (1) In any case where, after making a preliminary investigation under clause 7, MIB has decided that –

(a)   the case is one to which this Agreement applies, and

(b)   it is not one to which clause 13 applies,

MIB may notify the applicant of that decision and, instead of causing a full investigation and report to be made under clause 7, may make to the applicant an offer to settle his claim by payment of an award specified in the offer representing compensation assessed in accordance with clause 8 together, in an appropriate case, with interest thereon assessed in accordance with clause 9 and a contribution towards the cost of obtaining legal advice in respect of the making of the application.

(2)   Where an offer is made under paragraph (1), MIB shall send to the applicant a statement setting out –

(a)   the relevant evidence it has collected disclosing the circumstances in which the death, bodily injury or damage to property occurred, and

(b)   its reasons for the assessment of the award.

Settlement by accelerated procedure

27. (1) The applicant shall not later than 6 weeks after he receives an offer under clause 26 notify MIB of his acceptance or rejection thereof.

     (2) Where the applicant notifies MIB of his acceptance of the offer –

(a)   MIB shall not later than 14 days after receipt of the acceptance pay to the applicant the amount of the award, and

(b)   MIB shall be discharged from all liability under this Agreement in respect of the death, bodily injury or damage to property for which that payment is made.

     (3) In the event of the applicant failing to accept the offer within the specified period, the application shall be treated as one to which clause 7(1)(b) applies.

MISCELLANEOUS

Referral of disputes to arbitrator

28. (1) Any dispute between the applicant and MIB concerning a decision, determination or requirement made by MIB under the terms of this Agreement, other than a dispute relating to MIB's decision for which provision is made by clause 18, shall be referred to and determined by an arbitrator.

     (2) Where an applicant wishes to refer such a dispute to arbitration, he shall not later than 4 weeks after the decision, determination or requirement is communicated to him, give notice to MIB that he wishes the matter to be so resolved.

     (3) For the purposes of the Arbitration Act 1996 (where the arbitration is to be conducted in England and Wales) the arbitral proceedings are to be regarded as commencing on the date of such application.

     (4) Upon receipt of the applicant's notice MIB shall apply immediately to the Secretary of State for the appointment of an arbitrator and in the event of MIB failing to do so the applicant may make the application.

     (5) The Secretary of State shall, upon receiving the application for the appointment of an arbitrator to hear the appeal, appoint the first available member, by rotation, of a panel of Queen's Counsel appointed for the purpose of determining appeals under this Agreement (where the event giving rise to the death, bodily injury or damage to property occurred in England and Wales) by the Lord Chancellor or (where the

event giving rise to the death, bodily injury or damage to property occurred in Scotland) by the Lord Advocate and shall forthwith notify the applicant and MIB of the appointment.

(6) The applicant and MIB shall, not later than 4 weeks after receiving notification of the appointment of the arbitrator, submit to him a written statement of their respective cases with supporting documentary evidence where available.

(7) Subject to paragraphs (8) to (10), the arbitrator shall decide the appeal on the documents submitted to him under paragraph (6) and no further evidence shall be produced to him.

(8) The applicant may, by notice in writing given to the arbitrator and MIB not later than the date on which he submits the statement of his case, ask the arbitrator to determine the appeal by means of an oral hearing and shall submit to the arbitrator and MIB a written statement, with supporting documentary evidence where appropriate, in support of that request.

(9) The arbitrator shall in such a case seek the view of MIB on the need for an oral hearing and MIB may submit to the arbitrator and the applicant a written statement, with supporting documentary evidence where appropriate, in support of its view.

(10) If, after considering those written submissions, the arbitrator decides that an oral hearing is necessary to determine the dispute –

(a) the hearing shall be held in public unless the applicant requests that it (or any part of it) be heard in private;

(b) the hearing shall take place at a location –

(i) in England or Wales, where the event giving rise to the death, bodily injury or damage to property occurred in England or Wales and the applicant is resident in England or Wales,

(ii) in Scotland, where the event giving rise to the death, bodily injury or damage to property occurred in Scotland and the applicant is resident in Scotland, or

(iii) in England, Wales or Scotland in any other case,

which in the opinion of the arbitrator (after consultation with each of them) is convenient for both MIB and the applicant as well as for himself;

(c) a party to the hearing may be represented by a lawyer or other person of that party's choosing;

(d) a party to the hearing shall be entitled to address the arbitrator, to call witnesses and to put questions to those witnesses and any other person called as a witness.

(11) The arbitrator may, having regard to the subject matter of the proceedings and in an appropriate case, order that his fee or the costs of the proceedings (as determined according to clause 10(1)(b) of, and the Schedule to, this Agreement) or both his fee and those costs shall be paid by one party or allocated between the parties in such proportions as he thinks fit.

(12) Unless otherwise agreed, the decision, determination or requirement in respect of which notice is given under paragraph (2) shall stand unless reversed by the arbitrator.

Services of notices, etc, on MIB

29. Any notice required to be served on or any other notification or document required to be given or sent to MIB under the terms of this Agreement shall be sufficiently served or given sent by fax or by Registered or Recorded Delivery post to MIB's registered office

and delivery shall be proved by the production of a fax report produced by the sender's fax machine or an appropriate postal receipt.

Agents

30.   MIB may perform any of its obligations under this Agreement by agents.

Contracts (Rights of Third Parties) Act 1999

31.   (1)   For the purposes of the Contracts (Rights of Third Parties) Act 1999 the following provisions shall apply.

(2)   This Agreement may be –

(a)   varied or rescinded without the consent of any person other than the parties hereto, and

(b)   determined under clause 3(2) without the consent of any such person.

(3)   Save for the matters specified in paragraph (4), MIB shall not have available to it against an applicant any matter by way of counterclaim or set-off which would have been available to it if the applicant rather than the Secretary of State had been a party to this Agreement.

(4)   The matters referred to in paragraph (3) are any counterclaim or set-off arising by virtue of the provisions of –

(a)   this Agreement;

(b)   the 1996 Agreement;

(c)   the 1999 Agreement;

(d)   either of the agreements which were respectively superseded by the 1996 Agreement and the 1999 Agreement.

(5)   This agreement, being made for the purposes of Article 1(4) of Council Directive 84/5/EEC of 30th December 1983 –

(a)   is intended to confer a benefit on an applicant but on no other person, and

(b)   to confer such benefit subject to the terms and conditions set out herein.

Enforcement against MIB

32.   If MIB fail to pay compensation in accordance with the provisions of this agreement the applicant is entitled to enforce payment through the courts.

Transitional provisions

33.   The 1996 Agreement shall cease to have effect after 13 February 2003 but shall continue in force in relation to any claim arising out of an event occurring on or before that date.

IN WITNESS whereof the Secretary of State has caused his Corporate Seal to be hereunto affixed and the Motor Insurers' Bureau has caused its Common Seal to be hereunto affixed the day and year first above written.

SCHEDULE

MIB'S CONTRIBUTION TOWARDS APPLICANT'S LEGAL COSTS

1. Subject to paragraph 4, MIB shall pay a contribution towards the applicant's costs of obtaining legal advice determined in accordance with paragraph 2.
2. That amount shall be the aggregate of –

   (a) the fee specified in column (2) of the table below in relation to the amount of the award specified in column (1) of that table,

   (b) the amount of value added tax charged on that fee,

   (c) where the applicant has opted for an oral hearing under clause [28,]and

   (d) reasonable disbursements.

TABLE

Amount of the award (1)	Specified fee (2)
Not exceeding £150,000	15% of the amount of the award, subject to a minimum of £500 and a maximum of £3,000
Exceeding £150,000	2% of the amount of the award

3. For the purposes of paragraph 2 –

   'amount of the award' means the aggregate of the sum awarded by way of compensation and interest under clauses 8 and 9, before deduction of any reimbursement due to be paid to the Secretary of State for Work and Pensions through the Compensation Recovery Unit (CRU) of his Department (or to any successor of that unit), but excluding the amount of any payment due in respect of benefits and hospital charges.

   'reasonable disbursements' means reasonable expenditure incurred on the applicant's behalf and agreed between the applicant and MIB before it is incurred (MIB's agreement not having been unreasonably withheld) but includes Counsel's fees only where the applicant is a minor or under a legal disability.

4. The foregoing provisions of this Schedule are without prejudice to MIB's liability under the provisions of this Agreement to pay the costs of arbitration proceedings or an arbitrator's fee.

THE CORPORATE SEAL of THE SECRETARY OF STATE FOR TRANSPORT hereunto affixed is authenticated by:

Richard Jones
Authorised by the Secretary of State

THE COMMON SEAL of THE MOTOR INSURERS' BUREAU was hereunto affixed in the presence of:

James Read
Roger Snook
Directors of the Board of Management

Byford Louisy
Secretary

NOTES FOR THE GUIDANCE OF VICTIMS OF ROAD TRAFFIC ACCIDENTS

The following notes are for the guidance of anyone who may have a claim on the Motor Insurers' Bureau under this Agreement and their legal advisers. They are not part of the Agreement, their purpose being to deal in ordinary language with the situations which most readily occur. They are not in any way a substitute for reading and applying the terms of this or any other relevant Agreement, nor are they intended to control or influence the legal interpretation of the Agreement. Any enquiries, requests for application forms and general correspondence in connection with the Agreement should be addressed to:

Motor Insurers' Bureau
Linford Wood House
6–12 Capital Drive
Linford Wood
Milton Keynes
MK14 6XT

Tel: 01908 830001
Fax: 01908 671681
DX: 142620 MK10

1. INTRODUCTION – MIB'S ROLE AND APPLICATION OF THE AGREEMENT

1.1   The role of the Motor Insurers' Bureau (MIB) under this Agreement is to provide a safety net for innocent victims of 'hit-and-run' drivers or drivers who are otherwise untraceable. MIB's funds for this purpose are obtained from levies charged upon insurers and so come from the premiums which are charged by those insurers to members of the public.

1.2   MIB has entered into a series of Agreements with the Secretary of State and his predecessors in office for this purpose. Under each Agreement MIB has undertaken obligations to pay defined compensation in specific circumstances. There are two sets of Agreements, one concerned with victims of hit-and-run or otherwise untraceable drivers (the 'Untraced Drivers' Agreements) and the other with victims of identified but uninsured drivers (the 'Uninsured Drivers' Agreements). These Notes are addressed specifically to the procedures required to take advantage of the rights granted by the Untraced Drivers Agreements.

1.3   It is not always certain, however, which of those Agreements applies. In any case where there is doubt as to whether the driver of the vehicle (or his employer in a case where that employer may be vicariously liable) has been correctly identified it is advisable for the victim to apply under both the relevant Uninsured Drivers Agreement and this Agreement, following which MIB will advise which of them will, in its view, apply in the circumstances of the particular case.

1.4   In order to determine which of the Untraced Drivers Agreements is applicable to a particular victim's application, regard must be had to the date of the relevant incident. **This**

Agreement only applies in respect of claims arising on or after 14th February 2003.
Claims arising earlier than that are covered by the following Agreement:

1.4.1 Applications arising in respect of an incident occurring between 1st May 1969 and 30th November 1972 are governed by the Agreement between the Minister of Transport and the Bureau dated 21st April 1969.

1.4.2 Applications arising in respect of an incident occurring between 1st December 1972 and 30th June 1996 are governed by an Agreement between the Secretary of State for the Environment and the Bureau dated 22nd November 1972 though claims arising in respect of an incident occurring between 3rd January 1978 and 30th June 1996 are also governed by an Agreement supplemental to the 1972 Agreement made between the Secretary of State for Transport and the Bureau dated 7th December 1977.

1.4.3 Applications arising in respect of an incident occurring between 1st July 1996 and 13th February 2003 are governed by the Agreement between the Secretary of State for Transport and the Bureau dated 14th June 1996.

1.5 In all cases it is essential that an applicant has regard for any legal limitation period for commencement of proceedings. Should a decision under the relevant Agreement still be pending when the limitation date approaches the applicant should take legal advice as to whether proceedings should be issued against any person.

2. SCOPE OF THE AGREEMENT

2.1 The Agreement applies in a case where:

2.1.1 death, personal injury or damage to property has been caused as a result of the use of a motor vehicle on a road or in a public place in Great Britain (see clause 4(1)(a));

2.1.2 the circumstances were such that the liability of the unidentified person was a liability that was required to be covered by insurance or security under the Road Traffic Act 1988 (see clause 4(1)(c)); and

2.1.3 the person (or one of the persons) who apparently caused the death, injury or damage could not be identified (see clause 4(1)(d)).

2.2 An application to MIB **must** be made in writing and within the specified time limits and must contain adequate details (see clause 4(1)(e), (3) and (4) and clause 11(1)).

2.3 MIB will **not** accept an application:

2.3.1 for damage to property if the vehicle which allegedly caused the damage is unidentified (see clause 5(1)(a) and (3));

2.3.2 in certain cases where the vehicle involved was under the control of the Crown (see clause 5(1)(b));

2.3.3 in certain cases where the victim has assumed the risk (see clause 5(1)(c) and (f) and (2));

2.3.4 in cases of terrorism (see clause 5(1)(d));

2.3.5 in cases where the applicant has suffered no actual loss or has been compensated for any loss (see clause 5(1)(e) and (g)).

2.4 MIB's liability will in any case be limited where partial compensation is obtained from another source (see clauses 6(1) and (3) and 11(4)(d)) and will cease if full compensation is obtained from another source after the application is made (see clause 6(1) and (2)).

3. WHAT MIB PROMISES TO DO UNDER THE AGREEMENT

3.1   MIB will undertake an investigation of the application and make a report which may, according to the circumstances, be a preliminary or interim report (see clause 7(1), (3) and (4)).

3.2   MIB will determine whether or not to make an award according to whether it is satisfied on a balance of probabilities – the civil law burden of proof – that a court would have held the unidentified person liable to pay damages (see clause 7(2) and (6)).

3.3   If MIB decides to make an award the amount of compensation will be determined according to either the law of England and Wales or the law of Scotland depending upon where the incident occurred and will be calculated in the same way as a court would have calculated an award of damages (see clause 8). This obligation is subject to certain limitations, in particular:

3.3.1 There is an excess of £300 in respect of property damage (see clause 8(3)(a));
3.3.2 MIB's total liability in respect of property damage in any one incident, regardless of the number of persons affected, is limited to £250,000 less the excess applicable to each claimant (see clause 8(3)(c)).

3.4   MIB may make one or more interim awards (see clause 7(5)).

3.5   MIB will also –

3.5.1 in an appropriate case, pay interest on the compensation (see clause 9),
3.5.2 make a contribution towards the applicant's costs of obtaining legal advice on the application from a Solicitor, Barrister or Advocate (see clause 10 and the Schedule), and
3.5.3 pay reasonable disbursements agreed in advance with MIB, although MIB will not agree to pay for an expert's reports unless the report is disclosed (see the Schedule).

3.6   Notwithstanding those provisions, the Agreement does not prevent MIB from settling its obligations under the Agreement on the basis of a global sum representing compensation and interest (and possibly a contribution to the cost of legal advice also) if the applicant agrees. Furthermore, notwithstanding the restriction concerning Counsel's fees contained in the Schedule, MIB would consider paying all or some of those fees in a case involving a minor or other person under a disability.

3.7   For those cases which do not involve great complexity or a conflict of evidence, the Agreement provides for an accelerated settlement procedure if both parties agree (see clauses 26 and 27).

4. WHAT AN APPLICANT MUST DO

4.1   An applicant may be required by MIB, amongst other things, to –

4.1.1 supply written statements and other information relating to the incident or even make a statutory declaration;
4.1.2 be interviewed about the incident;
4.1.3 provide MIB where necessary with written authority enabling it to take steps to investigate the claim;
4.1.4 bring legal proceedings against an identified person who may be liable in respect of the death, injury or damage.

(See clause 11.)

4.2   MIB would be entitled to reject an application, either in whole or in part, if an applicant failed to comply with these conditions (see clause 31(5)(b)).

5.   JOINT LIABILITY

5.1   Where the death, injury or damage appears to have been caused partly by an unidentified person and partly by an identified person (or by two unidentified persons if the employer of one of them has been identified), the Agreement makes special provision about MIB's liability (see clauses 12 to 15).

5.2   MIB's liability will not in such cases exceed the liability of the unidentified person (or, as the case may be, the person whose employer has not been identified).

5.3   The Agreement contains provisions regarding what is to happen where a court judgement has been obtained against the identified person (the provisions differing according to whether it is satisfied or not and whether or not there is an appeal).

5.4   If judgement is obtained against an identified person who turns out to be uninsured the terms of the Uninsured Drivers Agreement will apply to determine MIB's liability.

6.   MIB'S DECISION AND PAYMENT OF THE AWARD

6.1   MIB will notify the applicant of its decision and set out the evidence on which it is based, findings of fact and the reasons for making it. MIB will also supply such further details as are relevant. (See clause 16.)

6.2   MIB may make the award –

6.2.1 as an interim award if it is based on an interim report (see clauses 7(5)(a) and 17(1)), or
6.2.2 in the form of a 'structured settlement' (see clause 17(2)), or
6.2.3 as a provisional award if the applicant satisfies it that there is a risk of his or her condition deteriorating further over a period of time (see clause 17(3) to (7)).

6.3   Unless there is an appeal the award will be made promptly (see clause 17(1)).

6.4   In an appropriate case where the applicant is a child or otherwise unable to manage his or her affairs, MIB may arrange for the award to be administered under a trust (see clause 25).

7.   APPEALS

7.1   An applicant may appeal against –

7.1.1 a decision to refuse to make an award, or
7.1.2 the amount of the award, or
7.1.3 a decision to refuse to make a provisional award, or
7.1.4 a proposal for a structured settlement.

(See clauses 18 and 20(2).)

7.2   Appeals must be made by notice in writing given within the period provided for in the Agreement (see clause 19). [MIB will provide a pro forma notice of appeal.]

7.3   MIB may, upon receipt of the notice of appeal –

7.3.1 if the applicant has provided additional evidence in support of the claim, cause a further investigation and report to be made (and if, upon completion of that further investigation, MIB decides to alter its decision it will notify the applicant accordingly);
7.3.2 apply to the Secretary of State for an arbitrator to be appointed to determine the appeal.

(See clause 20.)

7.4   Where there has been a further investigation and report, the applicant may either continue with the appeal or withdraw it although in appropriate cases MIB may undertake yet further investigations (see clause 20).

7.5   The arbitration procedure is set out in clauses 21 to 23. An applicant or even MIB may ask for an oral hearing. As regards the arbitration costs –

7.5.1 the arbitrator's fee is normally payable by MIB but there is provision for the arbitrator to order the applicant to pay where he holds that there were no reasonable grounds for the appeal (see clause 24(1) to (3));
7.5.2 where the applicant is successful MIB will, subject to any alternative order made by the arbitrator, pay a contribution of £500 per half day towards the cost of legal representation at an oral hearing (see clause 24(4)).

7.6   The Agreement also makes provision for the resolution of minor administrative disputes, e.g. about the reasonableness of requirements made by MIB under clause 11, to be referred to arbitration if they cannot be resolved more simply (see clause 28).

8.   MISCELLANEOUS

8.1   There are certain differences in procedure according to whether the incident occurred in England and Wales or in Scotland. These differences are referred to, where appropriate, in the Agreement.

8.2   In England and Wales the Contracts (Rights of Third Parties) Act 1999 applies subject to the provisions of clause 31.

APPENDIX 3

The 2008 Supplementary Agreement for uninsured drivers

THIS SUPPLEMENTARY AGREEMENT is made the 7th day of November 2008 between the SECRETARY OF STATE FOR TRANSPORT ('THE SECRETARY OF STATE') and the MOTOR INSURERS' BUREAU ('MIB') whose current registered office is Linford Wood House, 6–12 Capital Drive, Linford Wood, Milton Keynes MK14 6XT

IT IS HEREBY AGREED AS FOLLOWS:

1. This Agreement is supplementary to the Motor Insurers' Bureau (Compensation of Victims of Uninsured Drivers) Agreement made between the Secretary of State and the MIB dated 13th August 1999 ('the 1999 Agreement').
2. This Agreement shall come into force on the 7th day of November 2008 and applies to accidents occurring after midnight on that date onwards and from that time onwards the 1999 Agreement shall continue to apply in all respects save as provided for by the amendments set out in paragraph 3 below.
3. The 1999 Agreement shall be amended in the following respects:

    (a) The definition of 'specified excess' in Clause 1 is omitted.
    (b) In Clause 16(1) the word 'paragraphs' is replaced by the word 'paragraph'.
    (c) Clause 16(2) is omitted.
    (d) Clause 16(3) is omitted.
    (e) Clause 16(4) is replaced with the following Clause: '16(2) Where the property damage compensation in respect of any one accident exceeds £1million MIB's liability is limited to the sum of £1 million.'
    (f) In Clause 17 the words ', in addition to any sum deductable under clause 16,' are omitted.

IN WITNESS whereof the Secretary of State has caused his corporate seal to be hereunto affixed and the Motor Insurers' Bureau has caused its Common Seal to be hereunto affixed the day and year first above written.

THE CORPORATE SEAL of the SECRETARY OF STATE FOR TRANSPORT hereunto affixed is authenticated by:

....

Authorised by the Secretary of State

THE COMMON SEAL of the MOTOR INSURERS' BUREAU was hereunto affixed in the presence of:

Directors of the Board of Management ....

Secretary...

APPENDIX 4

The 2008 Supplementary Agreement for untraced drivers

THIS SUPPLEMENTARY AGREEMENT ('THIS AGREEMENT') is made the 30th day of December 2008 between the SECRETARY OF STATE FOR TRANSPORT ('THE SECRETARY OF STATE') and the MOTOR INSURERS' BUREAU ('MIB') whose registered office is Linford Wood House, 6–12 Capital Drive, Linford Wood, Milton Keynes MK14 6XT.

IT IS HEREBY AGREED AS FOLLOWS:

1. This Agreement is supplementary to the Untraced Drivers' Agreement made between the Secretary of State and MIB dated 7th February 2003 ('the 2003 Agreement').
2. This Agreement shall come into force on the 1st day of February 2009 and applies to accidents occurring after midnight on that date onwards and from that time onwards the 2003 Agreement shall continue to apply in all respects save as provided for by the amendments set out in paragraph 4 below.
3. The Interpretation Act 1978 shall apply for the interpretation of this Agreement as it applies for the interpretation of an Act of Parliament.
4. The 2003 Agreement shall be amended in the following respects:

    (a) In Clause 4(3)(a), for 'except in a case to which sub-paragraph (b) applies, the application must have been made not later than –' substitute 'the application must have been made within –';
    (b) Clause 4(3)(a)(i) is replaced with the following wording:

    '(i) subject to paragraph (a)(ii), the time limits provided for the victims of traced drivers bringing actions in tort by the Limitation Act 1980 (with regard to England and Wales) or the Prescription and Limitation (Scotland) Act 1973 (with regard to Scotland) in the case of a claim for compensation for death or bodily injury (whether or not damage to property has also arisen from the same event); but';

    (c) Clause 4(3)(b) is omitted, so that the existing Clauses 4(3)(c), 4(3)(d) and 4(3)(e) become (b),(c) and (d) respectively;
    (d) A new Clause 23(1)(f) is added with the following wording:

    '(f) determine, in like manner as a court, whether it would be equitable to allow the case to proceed having regard to the circumstances envisaged by section 33 of the Limitation Act 1980 (with regard to England and Wales) or section 19A of the Prescription and Limitation (Scotland) Act 1973 (with regard to Scotland);'.

In witness thereof the Secretary of State has caused his Corporate Seal to be hereunto affixed and the Motor Insurers' Bureau has caused its Common Seal to be hereunto affixed the day and year first written above

THE CORPORATE SEAL of THE SECRETARY OF STATE FOR TRANSPORT hereunto
authenticated by:

....

Authorised by the Secretary of State

THE COMMON SEAL of THE MOTOR INSURERS' BUREAU was hereunto affixed in
the presence of:

....

....

Directors of the Board of Management

....

Secretary

APPENDIX 5

The 2011 Supplementary Agreement for untraced drivers

THIS SUPPLEMENTARY AGREEMENT ('this Agreement') is made the 15th day of April 2011 between the SECRETARY OF STATE FOR TRANSPORT ('THE SECRETARY OF STATE') and the MOTOR INSURERS' BUREAU ('MIB') whose current registered office is Linford Wood House, 6–12 Capital Drive, Linford Wood, Milton Keynes MK14 6XT.

IT IS HEREBY AGREED AS FOLLOWS:

1. This Agreement is supplementary to the Untraced Drivers' Agreement between the Secretary of State and MIB dated 7th February 2003 ('the 2003 Agreement') as amended by the Supplementary Untraced Drivers' Agreement between the Secretary of State and MIB dated 30th December 2008 ('the Supplementary Agreement').

2. This Agreement shall come into force on the 15th day of April 2011 and applies to accidents occurring on or after that date. From that time onwards the 2003 Agreement (as amended by the Supplementary Agreement) shall continue to apply in all respects save as provided for by the amendments set out in clause 3 below.

3. The 2003 Agreement (as amended by the Supplementary Agreement) shall be further amended as follows:

   (a) In clause 1(1), after the definition of 'relevant proceedings', insert the following:

   > '"significant personal injury" means bodily injury resulting in death or for which 4 days or more of consecutive in-patient treatment was given in hospital, the treatment commencing within 30 days of the accident (evidence of such inpatient treatment will, in most cases, be a certificate of charges obtained from the Compensation Recovery Unit in accordance with the Health and Social Care (Community Health and Standards) Act 2003);'

   (b) In clause 1(1), after the definition of 'specified excess', insert the following:

   > '"specified property damage cap" means £1 million or such other sum as may from time to time be agreed in writing between the Secretary of State and MIB;'

   (c) Clauses 4(3)(b), (c) and (d) of the 2003 Agreement as amended by clause 4(c) of the Supplementary Agreement shall revert and become clauses 4(3)(c), (d) and (e) respectively. Notwithstanding clause 2 above, this amendment shall have retrospective effect and shall apply to accidents occurring after midnight on 1st February 2009.

   (d) Clause 5(1)(a) is replaced with the following wording:

   > '(a) where the applicant makes a claim for compensation in respect of damage to property caused by or arising out of the use of an unidentified vehicle unless –
   > (i) a claim for significant personal injury has been paid by MIB in respect of the same event, whether to the applicant or any other individual applicant; and
   > (ii) the loss incurred in respect of damage to property exceeds the specified excess;'

   (e) The wording of clause 5(3) is omitted (but notwithstanding this, the numbering of the subsequent clauses remains unchanged).

(f) Clause 8(3) is replaced with the following wording:

'(3) Where an application includes a claim in respect of damage to property, MIB's liability in respect of that claim shall be limited in accordance with the following rules –

(a) subject to paragraphs (b) and (c), MIB's liability to an individual applicant shall be the amount of the award calculated in accordance with clause 8(1);

(b) subject to paragraph (c), in any case in which damage to property is being claimed as a result of, or arising out of, the use of an unidentified vehicle, MIB's liability to an individual applicant shall, subject to Clause 5(1)(a), be the amount of the award calculated in accordance with clause 8(1), less the specified excess;

(c) in all cases, where MIB's total liability in respect of all property damage claims made in respect of any one event would otherwise exceed the specified property damage cap, MIB's total liability in respect of all such claims is limited to a sum equal to the specified property damage cap, less a sum equal to the specified excess multiplied by the number of applicants who have incurred loss due to property damage and whose claims are subject to the excess under (b) above.'

In witness whereof the Secretary of State has caused his Corporate Seal to be hereunto affixed and the Motor Insurers' Bureau has caused its Common Seal to be hereunto affixed the day and year first written above.

THE CORPORATE SEAL of THE SECRETARY OF STATE FOR TRANSPORT hereunto authenticated by:

Authorised by the Secretary of State

....

Print Name: PAUL O'SULLIVAN

Date: 15th April 2011

THE COMMON SEAL of THE MOTOR INSURERS' BUREAU was hereunto affixed in the presence of:

(1)..

Director of the Board of Management

(2)..

Secretary

Print Names:

(1) ASHTON WEST

(2) MOHAMMED HEMANI

Date: 14 APRIL 2011

APPENDIX 6

Memorandum of Understanding dealing with the effect of Byrne (a Minor) v. The Motor Insurers' Bureau and the Secretary of State for Transport [2008] EWCA Civ 574 on claims under the Untraced Drivers' Agreement

Following the Court of Appeal ruling in the court case of Byrne and the Secretary of State for Transport the government has asked the Motor Insurers' Bureau to reconsider those cases that were summarily rejected because the claim had not been made within the three years as required by the relevant Untraced Drivers Agreement and which fulfil certain conditions. The conditions are:

- The Claimant must have been the victim of an untraced driver in an accident occurring no earlier than 31 December 1988 (the deadline for the implementation of the Second Motor Insurance Directive – 84/5 EEC).
- The Claimant, the issue of limitation apart, must be entitled to an award under the relevant Untraced Drivers' Agreement.
- The Claimant must be or have been unable to claim compensation because of the 3 year time limit contained in the relevant Untraced Drivers' Agreement. For the avoidance of doubt, the MIB will not process a Claimant's application if any other exclusion applies or applied.
- Had the driver of the accident been traced, the limitation period (as provided for in the 1980 Act or in the 1973 Act as appropriate) for bringing a claim against that driver would have expired after 4 December 2003.
- The Claimant must be in time to bring a *Francovich* action against the Secretary of State, i.e. within 6 years from the date of accrual of the cause of action after the relevant limitation period under the 1980 Act or the 1973 Act as appropriate had expired. (For example, this would mean 6 years from age 21 in cases of personal injury sustained by a minor).

A formal arrangement has been entered into between the Department of Transport and the Motor Insurers' Bureau to reconsider those cases.

For more information please contact us.

APPENDIX 7

Memorandum of Understanding following the implementation of the Fifth EC Motor Insurance Directive and removing the excess payable by the claimant under the 1999 Uninsured Drivers' Agreement

UNTRACED DRIVERS' AGREEMENT 2003

Reclaiming the property damage excess for accidents with identified vehicles, or; Compensation for property damage for accidents with unidentified vehicles provided there is a payment for significant personal injury to any victim of the same accident.

As a result of the Fifth European Motor Insurance Directive, an excess of up to £300 should no longer apply to claims made to the Motor Insurers' Bureau ('MIB') in respect of compensation for damage to property caused by a driver of an identified vehicle under the Untraced Drivers' Agreement.

In addition, claims for property damage compensation under the Agreement, when the liable vehicle is unidentified, should be dealt with provided MIB has paid compensation for a significant personal injury to any victim of the same accident. 'Significant Personal Injury' is defined as that which results in death or for which 4 days or more of consecutive in-patient treatment was given in hospital, the treatment commencing within 30 days of the accident. However, compensation for these claims is subject to a £300 excess.

According to the Directive, these changes should have applied to accidents occurring on or after 11 June 2007.

An amendment to the Agreement between the Secretary of State for Transport and MIB, removed the right of MIB to apply an excess when settling claims arising from accidents with identified vehicles, and provided for compensation for property damage when a Significant Personal Injury payment is made to any victim of the same accident for which an unidentified vehicle is liable. However, these changes to the Agreement apply only to accidents that occurred on or after 15 April 2011.

For claimants whose claims for property damage relate to accidents occurring between 11 June 2007 and 14 April 2011 inclusive the Department for Transport has entered into a formal arrangement with the MIB in order to provide a quick and simple mechanism for redress.

This arrangement takes effect from 1 March 2012 and applies to accidents occurring between 11 June 2007 and 14 April 2011. It can be used for the benefit of victims whose claims as at 1 March 2012, are:

1. **Already submitted and ongoing**

2. Not yet submitted
3. Submitted and concluded

What you need to do depends on which of these categories your claim fits into:

1. Claims already submitted and ongoing

You do not need to take any action if you have already told MIB that you suffered some damage to your property. If you have only made a claim for injuries and now wish to add a property damage claim, see section 2 below.

MIB will review your claim and determine whether:

- In the event that the offending vehicle is identified, it can deal with your property damage element without applying an excess, or
- In the event that the offending vehicle is not identified and it has made a payment in respect of a Significant Personal Injury, it can deal with your property damage claim, subject to a £300 excess

These arrangements only apply where any claim for damage to property that has been made, was submitted to MIB within 9 months of the accident. In addition, all other terms, conditions and limitations of the Untraced Drivers' Agreement will apply.

If an award is made in these cases then the contribution to legal costs under the Agreement will be calculated and paid according to the total award made (including any additional payment made under this arrangement).

2. Claims not yet submitted

If you have not yet submitted a claim to MIB for damage to property and either of the following criteria applies:

- The offending vehicle is identified and your property damage claim is £300 or less or,
- The offending vehicle is not identified,

You must submit your claim to MIB on or before 30 November 2012.

All other terms, conditions and limitations of the Untraced Drivers' Agreement will apply.

If MIB decides to make a payment to you for damage to property, it will:

- In the event that the offending vehicle is identified, not apply any excess
- In the event that the offending vehicle is not identified and it has made a payment in respect of a Significant Personal Injury, include compensation for property damage, subject to a £300 excess
- In respect of contributions to legal costs:

  - Where the property damage claim is the first notification to MIB by the claimant in respect of the particular accident, it will make a contribution to legal costs in accordance with the terms of the Untraced Drivers' Agreement.
  - Where the property damage claim now made is an additional head of loss in respect of a previously submitted claim, MIB will pay the difference between the contribution that would have been paid had all heads of claim been submitted together and any actual contribution already paid.

3. Claims submitted and already concluded

If you only made a claim for injuries and now wish to make a property damage claim, see section 2 above.

However, if your claim has been concluded and either:

- MIB has deducted an excess of up to £300, or
- MIB have not paid your claim for property damage and the only reason was because the offending vehicle was not identified

you should contact MIB and ask it to review your claim. MIB will then make any further payment due or tell you why it cannot make a further payment.

In cases where an additional award is made in reimbursement of the excess in a previously closed case MIB will not make any additional contribution to legal costs. In unidentified vehicle cases where an additional award is made MIB will pay the difference between the contribution that would have been paid had all heads of claim been submitted together and any actual contribution already paid.

If you would like MIB to review your claim under these arrangements, you must contact them by 30 November 2012.

Anyone who believes they are entitled to benefit from these arrangements should contact MIB as follows:

Motor Insurers' Bureau
Linford Wood House
6–12 Capital Drive
Linford Wood
Milton Keynes MK14 6XT

Telephone Number: 01908 830001

Index